Patient and Public Involvement in Health and Social Care Research

Jurgen Grotz • Mary Ledgard
Fiona Poland

Patient and Public Involvement in Health and Social Care Research

An Introduction to Theory and Practice

palgrave
macmillan

Jurgen Grotz
Faculty of Medicine and Health
Sciences
University of East Anglia
Norwich, UK

Mary Ledgard
Norwich, UK

Fiona Poland
School of Health Sciences
University of East Anglia
Norwich, UK

Jurgen Grotz and Fiona Poland's involvement was supported by the National Institute of Health Research (NIHR) Applied Research Collaboration East of England (ARC EoE) programme. The views expressed are those of the authors, and not necessarily those of the NIHR, NHS or Department of Health and Social Care.

ISBN 978-3-030-55288-6   ISBN 978-3-030-55289-3   (eBook)
https://doi.org/10.1007/978-3-030-55289-3

This Palgrave Macmillan imprint is published by the registered company Springer Nature Switzerland AG.
The registered company address is: Gewerbestrasse 11, 6330 Cham, Switzerland

We dedicate this book to those taking part in patient and public involvement, who don't give up, who continue to try and who manage to also bring joy and love to doing it, often in difficult circumstances.

Preface

Before you go on to read the rest of this book, do ask yourself: *"Is this book right for me?"* We want to start now by explaining how you can find out.

This is a book about people coming together, involving patients and members of the public well, often in difficult circumstances, to make sure that health and social care research achieves good and relevant outcomes. If you would like to be a part of this, our book can help you to translate your interest in patient and public involvement (PPI) into practice that is both meaningful and achievable.

Before you start exploring further, you should know that involving patients and the public may not mean that everyone agrees all of the time. It may seem obvious that people whose lives may be affected by the research should help shape that research. But whether and how such involvement happens can be contentious—and the arguments may need to be heard! Some people don't welcome it at all, because they say it infringes academic freedom. Others say that only those who have lived experience are suitably qualified and therefore should have a leading role, rather than a minor role or none at all. And some see PPI as an unnecessary but obligatory drain on resources of money and time that must be managed efficiently to minimize disruption, bringing rules and regulations that make more bureaucracy rather than better PPI. Still others argue that disruption is a core function of PPI, so that rules and regulations are needed to support, not hinder it. Therefore, to take your PPI practice forward, you will need to recognise and address issues of diversity and disparities in power, and to be prepared to challenge inappropriate bureaucratic constraints.

This book aims to share, and encourage you to go on to add to, what is now seen as important in PPI by providing a comprehensive overview of current theory and practice on patient and public involvement in research. Its seven chapters cover the historical and conceptual background shaping PPI; a variety of ways of putting it into practice; what ethical issues need to be considered and critical perspectives on PPI including its potentially negative impacts. It also offers a step-by-step guide to planning PPI, including approaches to meaningful evaluation. Drawing on current literature, this book provides an essential reference work for all who want to better understand PPI in research and involvement practice. It includes a glossary of terms essential to this work. Many of the examples and much of the guidance we refer to are drawn from the National Health Service (NHS) in the UK before the 1990s, when responsibilities for health services were devolved to Wales and Scotland as well as Northern Ireland. Subsequent references are more often made to the NHS in England. The NHS in both periods took many steps and pioneered substantial guidance to promote PPI which has often since been referred to or drawn on by other countries worldwide in developing their own PPI. While we have provided examples of these other countries' activities and policies where possible, we have referred to NHS materials as they provide the currently most-cited, most comprehensive and most-reported and evaluated body of PPI activities and policies.

However, we cannot achieve meaningful involvement by reading a textbook alone. Our approach to PPI means moving away from ideas of *'seeking to involve others'* or *'being involved by others'* and towards *'each of us being involved with everyone else'*. This is about each of us taking personal responsibility for building the relationships that enable us to do so.

This presents us, the writers, with an awkward dilemma because this is, after all, a textbook. We have designed it for all people, including practitioners and researchers, who make inclusive involvement, in research happen, to do so competently. However, to make meaningful PPI happen we need not just to be competent in the practicalities of involvement, but also to be personally ready to commit to becoming involved and to take responsibility. Personal readiness can less easily be taught in a textbook as it relies on your own willingness to be or to become used to challenging and questioning yourself about what you are doing and thinking. We will help you by providing scenarios you can explore and key questions you can ask yourselves.

We suggest that before you start reading the rest of this book, you look again at your motivations to involve or be involved. If you only open the book to quickly find some buzzwords to add to a funding application where the funder has asked you to explain your approach to patient and public involvement, or if you are at the end of a project but now need to show some evidence of such involvement, this book won't help you very much.

We particularly encourage you to try and put yourselves in other people's shoes. This should be simple for the researchers and practitioners, to think like patients or the public, because they have all at one time or another been patients and are likely to be so more often as they become older. If, however, you are someone who sees your health or life experiences as relevant and motivating you to become involved in research and want to use this book to understand more about what you are letting yourself in for, try to briefly put yourself in the researcher's shoes. What do you think their needs and difficulties might be? If you are not ready to try to understand and to respect the perspectives of patients and the public, or to appreciate why researchers are researching, this book is not for you.

Finally, rather than *'involving'* or *'being involved by'*, we present all those involved as being *'involved with'*. This is very different. The methods and tools presented in this book rely on you bringing your personal commitment to those you seek to be involved with. If you are not prepared to ensure that everybody's time is spent wisely, to strictly avoid tokenism and to be committed to consistently preventing exclusion and promoting inclusion, this book will not fit your approach to practice.

This book will not offer you firm rules to tell you in advance what to do, nor will you be able to rely on this book to later say 'but they told me to do it that way' if something doesn't work out. This book will instead encourage you to apply your knowledge to question how involvement is happening as it happens, to include questioning yourself and your own role so that you can make your own assessment of what to do, with some confidence in yourself. You will therefore need to be able to make these crucial assessments and to take personal responsibility for your actions in making involvement happen. This means knowing about your motivation, perspective and commitment as presented in Fig. 1.

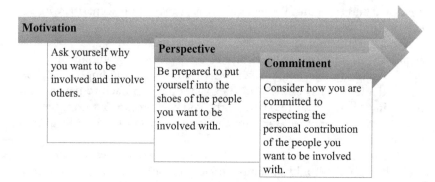

Fig. 1 Your motivation, perspective, commitment

Indeed, before starting to become involved in PPI, you may also want to look at some comments of others, which are freely available on the internet. One example is Peter Beresford's short video clip on '*How not to do service user involvement*'.

Having said all this, if you want to make PPI happen with meaning for all involved, we want to ensure that you can readily find plenty of evidence-based guidance in this book and importantly to also find enjoyment in the PPI process. It may not often be said, but if PPI is not at least a little bit enjoyable, people will not do it for long. PPI is about people being interested in coming together to learn and share lessons, in often difficult circumstances. Conviviality and respect must therefore be the most basic ingredients.

Norwich, UK   Jurgen Grotz
                                                              Mary Ledgard
                                                              Fiona Poland

Acknowledgements

We wish to thank all the many public, voluntary and community group members, the volunteers, health and social care professionals and researchers whose experiences and insights have inspired this work. While some of the conversations, dilemmas and ideas we are reporting are challenging, we have always found these to be instructive. We are now sharing some of what we have learned and hope this will lead to further discussion and new directions for collaborative research, and knowledge for inclusive involvement. We are also most grateful to our families and partners for their patience while we were writing this. We hope you will find it worthwhile and accessible.

CONTENTS

1 **Introduction**   1
  *1.1 What Are the Personal and Research Reasons
for Doing PPI?*   3
  *1.2 What Terminology—Words and Their Meanings—Can We
Agree for PPI?*   9
  1.3 Why Should We See PPI in Research as Volunteering?   14
  1.4 Where Is PPI Being Done in Research Activities?   16
  *1.5 How Can PPI Increase the Power of Patients and Public
to Shape Research?*   18
  1.6 Summary and Conclusions   18
  References   19

2 **Historical and Conceptual Background of Public
Involvement**   21
  2.1 Before the UK's NHS   25
  2.2 National Health Services Changes in 1948   29
  2.3 Diversifying Health Services   31
  *2.4 Twenty-First-Century Changes: Embedding PPI in Health
and Social Care and Research*   35
  2.5 Summary and Conclusions   37
  References   39

3   PPI in Research Practice   41
    3.1   The Principles of Patient and Public Involvement
          in Research   42
    3.2   Who to Be Involved With   43
    3.3   When to Be Involved   47
    3.4   How to Be Involved   51
    3.5   The Practicalities of Involvement   52
    3.6   What Can Go Wrong and How We Can Prepare to Deal
          with It   64
    3.7   Summary and Conclusions   65
    References   66

4   PPI in Research Ethics and Ethics in PPI   67
    4.1   Connecting Ethics, Everyday Actions and Research
          Activities   69
    4.2   Why do Laws Exist to Govern Ethics in Research   71
    4.3   What Is Lay Involvement in Research Governance?   73
    4.4   What Is Lay Involvement in Research Ethics?   74
    4.5   What Are the Ethics of Lay Involvement?   76
    4.6   Inclusion and Exclusion   78
    4.7   Ethics and Power   79
    4.8   Identifying and Deciding Ethical Issues in Practice   80
    4.9   Summary and Conclusions   82
    References   82

5   Critical Perspectives on Patient and Public Involvement
    in Research   85
    5.1   Do We Need Academic Freedom in Research?   89
    5.2   What Is a Service User Perspective?   92
    5.3   What Are Potentially Negative Impacts of PPI?   95
    5.4   Can We Agree on How to Evaluate PPI?   98
    5.5   Summary and Conclusions   100
    References   101

6   **The Coherence Model**   103
    6.1   Connecting   105
    6.2   Collaborating   120
    6.3   Complementing   128
    6.4   The Coherence Model of Good Practice in PPI
           Involvement—An Involvement Journey Checklist   137
    References   139

7   **Conclusion**   141
    References   148

Glossary   151

Index   161

About the Authors

Jurgen Grotz PhD, is the Director of the Institute for Volunteering Research (IVR) at the University of East Anglia, in the Faculty of Medicine and Health Sciences and a research fellow with the NIHR Applied Research Collaboration (ARC) East of England Inclusive Involvement in Research for Practice-Led Health and Social Care Theme. He has co-edited the Palgrave Handbook of Volunteering, Civic Participation, and Nonprofit Associations (2016).

Mary Ledgard Mary Ledgard's professional background was in policy analysis focusing on international politics and economics from the EU to China and North Korea. She moved on to work on service improvement in the public sector. On retiring, she decided to use her skills to put something back, serving as a trustee of Healthwatch Norfolk which gives a voice to local people on health and social care services. Today she focuses on working with the public sector on issues concerning older people and carers and is a relentless advocate of involving them in developing the services they need to live well and independently.

Fiona Poland is Professor of Social Research Methodology, leading the Inclusion Research Theme in the School of Health Sciences at the University of East Anglia (UEA), is UEA Lead for Volunteering Research, and co-leads the NIHR ARC East of England Inclusive Involvement in Research for Practice-Led Health and Social Care Theme. She is journal editor of Quality in Ageing and Older Adults.

ABBREVIATIONS

BMJ	British Medical Journal
CHC	Community Health Councils
GDPR	General Data Protection Regulations
HRA	Health Research Authority
NCVO	National Council for Voluntary Organisations
NHMRC	National Health and Medical Research Council (Australia)
NHS	National Health Service
NIHR	National Institute for Health Research
PPI	Patient and Public Involvement
PPIRes	Public and Patient Involvement in Research project
PPV	Patient and Public Voice
RDS	Research Design Service
REC	Research Ethics Committee
UKRI	UK Research and Innovation
UNCST	Uganda National Council for Science and Technology
VCSE	Voluntary, Community and Social Enterprise
VSSN	Voluntary Sector Studies Network
WHO	World Health Organisation

LIST OF FIGURES

Fig. 1.1   PPI where and how   17
Fig. 3.1   Patient and public involvement at the centre of the research cycle   48
Fig. 3.2   Roles and activities for PPI involvement in research   51
Fig. 6.1   Coherence Model   104
Fig. 6.2   Basic logic model   132

LIST OF TABLES

Table 3.1   Groups to help find people to involve as members of the public or patients   45

Table 3.2   Accessibility topics to consider for involvement   56

Table 3.3   Collaborative practice based on shared understandings of decision-making processes, roles, information and consequences   60

Table 3.4   Communication practices to support involvement   60

Table 3.5   Practices in being involved in evaluating processes and products of research   61

Table 3.6   Practicalities of payments for involvement   63

Table 4.1   Identifying and deciding ethical issues in practice: key questions to ask   81

Table 6.1   Example of objectives relating to an outcomes framework specific to the development of PPI in a research project   133

Table 6.2   Example of output measures relating to an outcomes framework   134

Table 6.3   Involvement checklist   138

LIST OF CASE EXAMPLES

Case Example 1   Alms Houses   23
Case Example 2   Setting the Scope   50
Case Example 3   Working with Disabled People   53
Case Example 4a   Pregnant Women and Smoking   69
Case Example 4b   Pregnant Women and Smoking, the PPI Member View   70
Case Example 4c   Pregnant Women and Smoking, Cultural Influences   71
Case Example 5   Funding Criteria   91
Case Example 6   The failed symposium on collaboration and inclusion   97
Case Example 7   Engaging Carers   110
Case Example 8   Being Overwhelmed by Experts   115
Case Example 9   Effect of Meetings on Health   120
Case Example 10   Rights of Volunteers   125

CHAPTER 1

Introduction

Since at least the 1960s, disabled people, people living with challenging conditions, people living in disadvantaged neighbourhoods and members of groups seen as *different*, have highlighted that their needs for health and social care services cannot be well understood or evidenced unless they are involved in producing knowledge about the needs of their communities for use in research and for themselves. Involving patients and the public in health and social care research is therefore vital for providing services and research that can be recognised as relevant to and connected with people's lives and wellbeing.

Respecting people as citizens who can play their part fully as members of society is a key moral issue. Denying access to health and social care services and to shaping those services constrains people's ability to act for themselves and for others, and to be treated equitably. It is also now required by law in the UK, in many European countries, and on other continents.

Because people's lives and needs are so different and because we are still finding out about these by working and talking with each other, we cannot know what they are in advance of planning research. Nor can we decide in advance what are the best ways to build such involvement, particularly since being a patient and public involvement (PPI) representative must be a voluntary activity. This means that the most suitable approach is not something we automatically agree on. It is something where we can build on lessons from the different experiences of ourselves and others to date

© The Author(s) 2020
J. Grotz et al., *Patient and Public Involvement in Health and Social Care Research*, https://doi.org/10.1007/978-3-030-55289-3_1

to work together to decide what kinds of voluntary patient and public involvement may be useful to each of us to apply and to develop. We are therefore writing this book, drawing on our different experiences of supporting patient and public involvement in research, as volunteers and researchers, so as to provide some definitions of what it is, reasons why it should be done, how it can be done and what resources can help us to do it well.

A clear and compelling challenge we must address is how to ensure that we comprehensively involve the range of different individuals and groups we need, while they are also acting as volunteers. This means that PPI must be inclusive and be shown to be inclusive. Again, we cannot assume in advance that we know how to work inclusively until researchers and community members are talking, sharing and revising their views.

This book is therefore designed to help readers to find their own way, to make their own decisions about and to take responsibility for identifying what is important and useful for supporting PPI that works for them, in order to produce good evidence for designing health and social care and to guide collaborative and voluntary relationships to achieve this. In this way, you can recognise your responsibilities and means of being responsible for good PPI practice in the research you are contributing to.

It is important to remember that research into health and social care covers a number of very different types of health topics, groups and places, ranging from medicines and hospital treatment to care provision for those living with long-term conditions and the public health of particular communities. Research within each of these areas will need to take account of different cultures and practices of people working in and using them. PPI that can bring useful insights in each case will mean taking additional account of the kinds of PPI needed, the different skills it will call for, and what this will mean for engaging with and supporting PPI.

In this chapter, we start by setting out the basics you should know to get started in supporting or actively developing the involvement of patients and the public in research, whether as a PPI representative, a researcher or a member of a group commissioning research. At the end of this chapter, you should know how to define for yourself what patient and public involvement is, how it is talked about, the reasons for doing it, and what roles it can play in research. This will include appreciating different viewpoints about this role and what means people have to express their viewpoints on becoming involved in research. It will be clear by now that our approach should also equip you to question PPI guidance that seems to assume widespread consensus about the issues involved. If such guidance exists, it is unlikely to have recognised the different experiences and views of groups that need to be involved. Assuming rather than building such consensus can bury diverse points of view or close off ways of expressing them. To work inclusively therefore means that you will need also to take responsibility for being continuously open to the possibility that other people's views and the ways they express them may be different from your own or what you have experienced so far.

We will now look more closely at questions to help us work out key features shaping PPI in our own situation and more widely:

- What are the personal and research reasons for doing PPI?
- What terminology—words and their meanings—can we agree for PPI?
- Why should we see PPI in research as volunteering?
- Where is PPI being done in research activities?
- How can PPI increase the power of patients and the public to shape research?

1.1   What Are the Personal and Research Reasons for Doing PPI?

Supporting PPI cannot be a tick box exercise existing only as words on paper rather than as shared understandings and actions in practice. We need to identify appropriate reasons for supporting it. We need to understand how to ensure that these reasons are embodied in the activities we personally undertake, and why we want to and should involve people in shaping it. Exercise 1.1 gives you a chance to think about a working example.

Exercise 1.1
You are setting up a new project to find out how to improve community services for disabled people. Why may you want patient and public representatives to be involved in the project?

In carrying out this exercise you may want to think about how disabled people think, and can be thought about, as members of the community in question, and who can bring relevant information to shape and give access to community services that include the groups involved.

Whether PPI happens will depend on the reasons why we think it should be done. There are at least five types of argument for supporting PPI within health and social care research:

- The theory-based (epistemological) argument—who can know best?
- The methodological argument—how do we gain more accurate and relevant knowledge to achieve better results from research?
- The moral argument—what are the democratic and ethical reasons for doing PPI?
- Funder requirements
- Legal requirements—what do laws tell us our own and others' responsibilities are in doing PPI?

The theory-based (epistemological) argument—who can know best?

One of the most compelling arguments for involving patients and the public is that they are especially well-placed to develop and share relevant knowledge of what is needed and what does or does not work. This is often based on their experience as service users. Service user is both a descriptive and a political term. Some researchers suggest that only a 'significant minority' would like to be referred to as service users (Simmons et al. 2010). Peter Beresford is a mental health service user and researcher who has tested out and campaigned for these arguments with service users and organisations for many years. He has published 'A Short Theory of Knowledge Distance and Experience' for the service user organisation 'Shaping Our Lives'. Beresford argues that we must value 'experiential knowledge' rather than simply dismiss it as 'non-scientific', because knowledge created without the insights available from evidence based on experience is fundamentally flawed.

> *The greater the distance between direct experience and its interpretation, then the more likely resulting knowledge is to be inaccurate, unreliable and distorted.* (Beresford 2003: 4)

However, such an argument directly challenges the values of academic scientific methods of evidence-building which mainly prioritise remaining neutral and objective, and keeping a distance between researchers, research and those whose lives may be affected by research findings on a topic. The involvement in research of a person with a close interest in its results may be seen as being likely to lead to biased results, so many academics may resist mixing research to build unbiased evidence and 'interested' experience. We will revisit how these issues may be dealt with in supporting and developing PPI, translating them into real-life motives and decision-making in the sections and chapters that follow, including those on research ethics.

The methodological argument—how do we gain more accurate knowledge to achieve better results from research?

While we may not agree on whether individual groups will have more or less relevant or unbiased experience to shape knowledge, we may agree that some people will have more accurate and detailed knowledge of living with conditions and support services to help us fine-tune what we already know and to design services that take this into account. Patients can offer insights and stories which are based on their direct experience of a particular condition, and taking these views into account will improve the focus and quality of the research and increase its connections with people's lives. Such connections may be strengthened if some of the evidence is gained through collaborations with peer researchers. The National Institute for Health Research (NIHR) Research Design Service (RDS) which supports health and social care researchers across England, for example, offers this advice.

> The contributions of patients can be extremely valuable, providing alternative views from those of the research team or NHS staff. Patients are able to make judgements based on their understanding of their condition and may have different aspirations and thoughts about health outcomes that health care professionals and researchers may not have considered. (NIHR RDS 2014: 6)

This is different to the epistemological argument above as it simply suggests that the work that researchers do should be informed by the details of people's experience including their concerns, culture, language and education. This kind of detailed knowledge can be brought by PPI representatives to help make patient leaflets easier for non-researchers to read and understand, or to explain where to locate and build collaborative relationships between researchers and other groups of people who may take part in the research or want to know about the research findings and its likely effects. The morality and ethics involved in research, which comes from involving people, can be a part of the methodological argument.

The moral argument—what are the democratic and ethical reasons for doing PPI?

Research aiming to produce findings which affect people's lives cannot make a difference unless it has public support; and it will not gain that support if it cannot be shown to be relevant and beneficial rather than harmful to those affected during or through the research. Where such research aims to evidence the specific usefulness of health and social care services which are publicly funded or publicly regulated, we need to ensure there is democratic agreement on what topics and methods are most important and relevant. Undertaking PPI provides a way to build democratic participation and agreement in shaping public services and evidence, and to demonstrate that this level of involved participation is being actively promoted. This can be seen increasingly in the statements of formal principles, policies and procedures developed by research funders, service providers, commissioners and other public and private organisations involved in the UK and in other countries.

We can see an example of a national policy following such principles in the National Health Service (NHS) Constitution for England (2015) which opens with the sentence "*The NHS belongs to the people*". As the NHS is publicly owned, it is widely acknowledged that the public will demand forms of democratic participation so as to actively shape it and patient and public involvement is seen as an important form of such participation; such involvement can be seen to be central to planning, informing and decision-making.

> *You have the right to be involved, directly or through representatives, in the planning of healthcare services commissioned by NHS bodies, the development and consideration of proposals for changes in the way those services are provided, and in decisions to be made affecting the operation of those services.* (NHS 2015: 9)

It is fair to say that such a democratic approach is not yet embedded in how the NHS or social care services work on a day-to-day basis. This is complicated further in countries with devolved sovereignty such as the UK where, for instance, there is now not only an NHS for England but also for separately governed health services in Wales, Scotland and Northern Ireland. Although there are now many more examples than there used to be from primary care patient participation groups to carer support groups, there is still a long way to go. NHS and social care leaders may not always provide wholehearted organisational support to the policy, nor can patients and the public easily access the time, resources and incentives to participate. For example, a substantial part of the problem is that more often than not involvement activities take place in working hours. For PPI to happen more routinely, people will need to see that their involvement will actually make a difference. To achieve this, good practice in PPI is essential as we will find out in the coming chapters.

The importance of PPI in ensuring research is both relevant and also ethical is widely acknowledged by many of the key research funders in health and social care who now explicitly require PPI in the projects or programmes they fund. Ethics is about ensuring that people taking part in research or affected by its findings are well-informed about any potential harms or benefits and can give voluntary consent to take part. PPI can help provide the understanding of people's culture, language and education needed to ensure these ethical principles are applied for different places and communities. This is discussed in more detail in Chap. 5.

The legal requirements—what do laws tell us our own and others' responsibilities are in doing PPI?

A wide range of legal duties must be observed by anyone involved in carrying out research, including PPI representatives contributing to research, but also research teams working with PPI representatives. These include observing any laws that apply worldwide to securely handling confidential data and the personal details of anyone connected with the research (in the UK, this is covered by the Data Protection Act (2018)), and any government policies relating to safeguarding vulnerable participants, such as in genetics or the rights to equality and diversity of specific groups. Laws apply to standards in research such as preventing fraud, breaking into others' information systems or gaining information through coercion. There are legal rights governing intellectual property involved in research designs and the products of research. Legal restrictions have also been set preventing research on some types of topic. Where PPI members of research teams are involved in taking responsibilities for aspects of research planning, activities or management, they will need to follow the same legal duties as anyone else involved in delivering the research and will need to be equipped to know what these are and also what is involved in meeting them.

In England, the Health and Social Care Act (2012) placed legally binding duties on the NHS and on clinical commissioning groups to *"make arrangements to secure that individuals to whom the services are being or may be provided are involved (whether by being consulted or provided with information or in other ways)"* (Paragraph 13Q: 22). This Act required every higher-level local authority to set up a Health and Well-Being Board. The aim is to build partnership working between all key stakeholders to improve the commissioning and delivery of services across the NHS and local government. The local Healthwatch, a statutory organisation that provides the consumer voice of the local population, is a member by right. These boards may involve patients and the public in various ways such as through consultations or by setting up working groups which may include voluntary sector representatives to ensure that local communities shape local health and social care services, or regional public health networks.

These duties appear to extend to the Health Research Authority (HRA), which is also linked to the Department of Health but without corresponding statutory duties. However, as with all UK health organisations, the HRA has confirmed its commitment to an environment providing PPI opportunities within the UK policy framework for health and social care research, including *"to get involved in its design, management, conduct and dissemination, and are confident about doing so"* (Health Research Authority 2017a: 4).

While we can expect these duties to extend to the NIHR, in England, this is not explicitly stated. The NIHR is one of the significant funders of research in health and social care. It is mostly funded by the Department of Health and Social Care and distributes those funds mainly through working directly with the NHS and universities.

The legal requirements for involving individuals and groups extend to involving people in their own health and social care. This also includes being involved in commissioning such services, and specific guidance is available for commissioning organisations.

Professional standards run parallel to legal requirements and are covered in Chap. 5.

Key Questions 1.1
What are your personal reasons for involving patients and the public in your current work in research?
What other reasons may there be for involving patients and the public in your current work in research?

1.2 What Terminology—Words and Their Meanings—Can We Agree for PPI?

If we want to identify, understand and collaborate on PPI, we need to know what words will help us do this. Unfortunately, we don't all agree! Individual words may be used to refer to very different things, especially when we may be bringing together different experience and motivations to getting involved. Or we may well use different words when we are talking about the same things in practice. So if we are to work well together in PPI, we need to be aware of this to avoid misunderstandings.

We will now have a look at some of the key terms currently used. You will by now recognise that there cannot be general standardised agreement on what each one means and that you will have to clarify which ones people are using in different contexts and how they are using them. Particularly important here are the terms 'involvement', 'engagement' and 'participation'; again there can be no authoritative or lasting way to define these in a way that applies in every context. The recently developed NHS Patient and Public Participation Policy (2017b) is expressed in ways that can be tailored to different groups and contexts:

> *Participation (sometimes referred to as engagement or involvement) can take place in a variety of ways, for example through social media, voluntary community and social enterprise (VCSE) organisations, elected representatives, formal consultations and meetings. NHS England is committed to taking an approach that is appropriate to the situation and the needs of the people it is seeking to engage.* (NHS England 2017b: 6)

The UK National Institute for Health Research funded organisation INVOLVE established in 1996, and not to be confused with a UK public participation charity 'Involve' established in 2003, is one of still only a very few government-funded bodies in the world to bring together PPI experience and insights to promote it as vital to research priorities, processes and products. This organisation makes a distinction between the three terms, allocating a more specific meaning to each. They define 'involvement' as where members of the public are active in research projects and organisations and offer as examples:

- *as joint grant holders or co-applicants on a research project*
- *identifying research priorities*
- *as members of a project advisory or steering group*
- *commenting and developing patient information leaflets or other research materials*
- *undertaking interviews with research participants*
- *user and/or carer researchers carrying out the research. (NIHR INVOLVE 2012: 7)*

How quickly these terms and definitions may change is illustrated by an announcement by the National Institute for Health Research (NIHR) that from April 2020 the 'NIHR centre for patient and public involvement, engagement & participation and research dissemination' would be hosted by a private company, LGC Limited, which, as the centre's name suggests, will be co-ordinating and defining key components of PPI.

Exercise 1.2 provides an example where you can consider whether you can use the NIHR INVOLVE definitions of involvement to decide whether this is an example of a group that is involved in shaping research.

Exercise 1.2
You have invited members of a patient support group for people with arthritis to discuss your research proposal to examine the effects of falls on their lives. How are they being involved in this research?

'Participation', for INVOLVE, is concerned exclusively with people being recruited as research subjects in clinical trials or social research, for example to complete research questionnaires. In contrast, 'engagement', for INVOLVE, concerns disseminating academic information through activities such as science festivals and general awareness raising about academic work.

It is worth noting that INVOLVE includes the dissemination of study findings to research participants in its definition of 'engagement', while often describing this dissemination elsewhere as an integral part of 'involvement' (NIHR INVOLVE 2012). This example highlights how definitions are used in varying ways even by the organisation working most closely with PPI members and how such definitions cannot remain fixed. The way these terms are used in the context of groups being involved in research at different times and for different purposes will remain inconsistent and very likely to change over time.

Unfortunately, the confusion does not become much clearer when we go on to look at the terms used to describe people who are involved. Are they 'service users', 'lay representatives', 'lay voices', 'public voice representatives', 'patient and public involvement (PPI) representatives', 'experts by experience' or 'stakeholders'? NHS England again applies these flexibly:

> *Patient and Public Voice (PPV) Partners* – *'people who are willing to share their perspective and experience with NHS England to inform health services in a range of different ways'* – *in its work. PPV Partners include patients, service users, carers, families and other members of the public. PPV Partners may also be referred to as people participating in 'service user involvement', 'lay representatives', 'lay voices', 'public voice representatives' or 'patient and public involvement (PPI) representatives'.* (NHS England 2017a: 4)

This may suggest to us that a way to start deciding how to find and use appropriate language would be to discuss and agree with people being involved in a particular piece of research how they would like to be described. This may sometimes mean referring to their role, for example lay representative; in other cases, it may be referring to the contribution they plan to make. Clarity and transparency of intentions need to be reflected in the terminology you use from the outset. We will revisit this issue in more detail in later chapters.

The central concern of this book is of course 'Patient and Public Involvement in Research', so for the moment, we will proceed by providing an outline of some key terms we, the authors, aim to use in particular ways, explaining more about our reasons for suggesting these over the chapters that follow. We will take care to beware of terms which may suggest people are involved and shaping decisions, but which, if we are using them accurately, mean people are merely being informed about or are watching other people take decisions.

Patient and Public

A starting point for defining patients and the public is to ask the question who they may be. Most current descriptions are as inclusive as possible, recognising that virtually everybody will be a patient at some time.

> *The term 'patients and the public' includes everyone who uses services or may do so in the future, including carers and families. People who use health and care services may be referred to as 'experts by experience'.* (Patient and Public Participation Policy, NHS England 2017b: 6)

Thus, the term seems to imply that it includes both those who carry out research, or involve others, and those who are involved. When we use the term in this book we too want to be comprehensive, but to go one step further by recognising that all those who set out to involve will also be and have experience as patients and members of the public and so will have their own insights from that perspective. That raises the question: is there a key distinction between those involving and those being involved? Some guidance suggests that those being involved have no professional role in the context where involvement is being developed and applied, offering a distinction between researchers in health and social care and health and care professionals on the one hand, and on the other, patients, carers and other community-based partners. However, such a distinction raises several problems. For example, we know of academics with health conditions who have been invited on panels as PPI representatives because of their condition; yet they clearly also have professional experience which they cannot simply leave behind at the door. Another example is people who represent voluntary and charitable organisations; they may be paid staff, trustees or volunteers, and they may again bring professional expertise. The NHS England guidance recognises that when working with representatives of other organisations, especially from small, user-led organisations, researchers may need to support them if they are otherwise unable to take part (NHS England 2017a, 11). So, 'patient and public' is potentially everybody, and we should be cautious about starting with too rigid a definition of what we need, but decide what is appropriate, respectful and inclusive when involving people in such research. This raises an important question especially in relation to those marginalised groups who want to speak for themselves. We will address this question in Chap. 5.

Involvement
Involvement is when patients and the public move from being unquestioning recipients of services to being involved citizens, not just in decisions about their own care but in the planning and delivery of care for all. Of course, there are many forms of involvement and we need to be conscientious in describing the context and purpose of any particular instance of involvement if we are to understand and fully share what we really mean. It is simply not good enough to refer to the word involvement and leave it at that.

Like NHS England, we view all PPI representatives in health and social care as volunteers. This raises important questions, for example, about payments which, according to a definition from the United Nations International Year of the Volunteer, are not completely excluded: "...*the activity should not be undertaken primarily for financial reward, although the reimbursement of expenses and some token payment may be allowed...*" (as quoted in Ellis Paine et al. 2010: 9) We will deal with these questions in Sect. 1.3.

We also argue that involvement applies 'in both directions'. By this we mean that involvement does not rely on a formal invitation but may be on the initiative of an individual patient or member of the public. Involvement can be about taking an active part in shaping health and social care as a volunteer of a local Healthwatch or of a community organization overseeing care services. It can also be as a volunteer on a hospital ward or in a hospice, having freely chosen to actively provide services for others and by doing so changing and monitoring those very services.

Patient and Public Involvement
This term is currently widely used but is also changing. It does not seem to have a firmly agreed definition, and needs to be tailored to and agreed in different contexts. It does not by itself guarantee a focus on involvement that is inclusive. When we use the term in this book we refer to the process of patients and the public moving from being unquestioning recipients of services to involved citizens not just in decisions about their own care but in the planning and delivery of care for all.

Patient and Public Involvement in Research
NIHR uses the following very broad definition: "*research being carried out 'with' or 'by' members of the public rather than 'to', 'about' or 'for' them*" (NIHR INVOLVE 2012: 6). When we use the term in this book, it flows from the way we use Patient and Public Involvement. Thus, Patient and Public Involvement in Research is when people move from being unquestioning subjects of research to being involved members of a group which undertakes research; patients and the public are involved in this group in a voluntary capacity to improve the created knowledge and strengthen the methodology. In such research patients and the public will have physical, psychological and communication access to all relevant aspects of research and the respective roles, and the research meets legal requirements and professional standards.

Key Questions 1.2
Who should define what the terms mean?
What world-view is expressed by the definitions? Think particularly about the terms 'service user', 'expert by experience' and 'PPI representative'.

1.3   WHY SHOULD WE SEE PPI IN RESEARCH AS VOLUNTEERING?

Perhaps this question is not one you expected. You may ask what volunteering has got to do with PPI.

Firstly, it important to note that official UK health service guidance, both for the NHS services and the Health Research Authority, refers to those involved in PPI as volunteers. A Health Research Authority annual report (2017b) refers to "*1,000 or so volunteers who serve on the RECs [Research Ethics Committees], the National Research Ethics Advisors' Panel (NREAP), the Public and Patient Involvement Panel ... who give their time freely to support the HRA and our work*" (ibid: 5) and in a later report, volunteers are also described as "*part of our patient and public involvement network*" (Health Research Authority 2019: 6).

The NHS guidance on volunteer recruitment includes as specific examples of volunteer roles in NHS provider organisations "*expert patients*" and "*GP patient participation group*" (NHS England 2017c: 5).

We also know that PPI is recognised as relevant in all aspects of health and social care, from commissioning to service improvements, from oversight to governance. Widely known examples of involvement activities in the UK health services organisations are: in Healthwatch England and local Healthwatch organisations where members of local communities seek information relevant to them and provide feedback on their health experiences; in clinical commissioning group where they are consulted; as volunteers in the work of NHS organisations and charities; and through NIHR INVOLVE, the body officially funded to promote PPI.

Examples of PPI roles include:

Role 1: People choose to respond or comment on open access engagement opportunities, for example responding to online surveys. Expenses Category A (no financial support from NHS England). No expenses can be claimed.

Role 2: PPV Partner is invited to attend workshops / events / focus groups on a 'one off' basis. Expenses Category B (out-of-pocket expenses are covered or reimbursed).

Role 3: PPV Partner is a member of regular working group meetings. Expenses Category B (out-of-pocket expenses are covered or reimbursed).

Role 4: PPV partners are in senior PPV Expert Advisor roles that demonstrate strategic and accountable leadership and decision making activity. Expenses Category C (out-of-pocket expenses are covered or reimbursed AND an involvement payment is offered). (NHS England 2017a: 8)

For example, in its Annual Report 2016–17, Healthwatch England thanks its 4700 volunteers who *"gave up their time to support our work"* (Healthwatch 2017).

Importantly, all these roles are voluntary: unpaid and freely chosen. So here, NHS England insists in its guidance that even those involved in 'Expert Advisor' roles are 'volunteers and not employees', despite this same guidance emphasising that senior 'Expert Advisors' should be paid 'at least equal to the National Minimum Wage'. Rates for 'involvement payments' are currently set at £150 per day/meeting or £75 per half day. Ensuring this is a volunteer role is vital if people undertaking it are going to be seen to make independent contributions which take into account or seek to represent the views and interests of other groups of people beyond services or policymakers.

NHS England provides detailed guidance on how its approximately three million volunteers (NHS England 2017c) can contribute and be respectfully and safely supported. The need for this was reinforced by the Lampard Inquiry which investigated matters relating to the widespread abuse by Jimmy Saville through his volunteer access to service users, staff, services and information.

However, what links NHS guidance on volunteer involvement to the practice of public involvement in general and in health and social care research in particular is often less clear. At times, what happens can seem to directly contradict the NHS's own standards of involvement and its stated ambition. For example, the NIHR Standards of Involvement aim to provide *"clear, concise benchmarks for effective public involvement alongside indicators against which improvement can be monitored"* (NIHR 2018: 2). However, while they are described as being based on results from a public consultation, they remain vague. They do not clearly reflect strongly argued and evidenced concepts and values which can build trust, for example, amongst currently excluded groups such as homeless people or those in the criminal justice system. These people may find it difficult to recognise how their needs and views are being taken into account through purposeful and independent involvement:

> *They are not designed as rules, or to provide fixed ideas about public involvement in research. They aid setting realistic expectations, encourage improvement and achieve excellence in public involvement in research. Over time they can provide organisations with minimum expectations of public involvement in research. They can be tailored to suit your situation, for example; the type of research you are doing, the amount of resource (money, people, skills) you have, and the purpose of your public involvement in research.* (NIHR 2018: 4)

PPI is a form of volunteering; indeed, it is many forms of volunteering. It is therefore relevant and important for us to apply wider lessons from good practice in involving volunteers to inform the good practice in PPI we aim to promote through this book.

1.4   WHERE IS PPI BEING DONE IN RESEARCH ACTIVITIES?

Undertaking PPI means being involved in specific research activities. Again, we need to be aware that different kinds of research activities may be but are not uniformly planned as part of developing particular research programmes. These include allocating funding; regulating areas of research such as overseeing ethics; or managing programmes or individual research projects and research team members; recruiting participants; collecting and analysing data, and writing reports of findings. As we have seen in Sect. 1.1 on reasons for supporting PPI, legal requirements to do this seem to extend to research; and methodological, moral and epistemological reasons clearly also apply. In Chap. 4 on PPI in research ethics, we will also see areas where PPI is formally required to oversee ethical research design and practice. Much current guidance suggests that PPI needs to be considered as part of research in all areas, at all levels and all stages, from deciding what research gets funded, to providing researchers with information about and for patients, and appropriate ways to communicate with them and the public (see Fig. 1.1). However, there are few rules which set out clearly whether any of this is compulsory and if so how best to do it.

However, this is only part of the picture. The National Institute for Health Research Annual Report states that its funding in 2015/2016 led to 13,282 publications, naming specifically the British Medical Journal (BMJ) amongst others (National Institute for Health Research 2016: 23). For many of these publications, authors have had to meet formal requirements. For instance, from 2014 the editors of the leading British research journal for family medical practitioners, the BMJ, have formally required authors of research papers to document if and how they have involved patients in setting the research question(s), the outcome measures, the study design and implementation, and in disseminating its results. A literature review reported that in the twelve months following the introduction of the policy, only 11% of the publications they had covered reported on any patient and public involvement activity. Of these, only a third had acknowledged the contributions of PPI volunteers and only one in ten had included any PPI volunteers as co-authors (Price et al. 2018). It is fair to say publications are still in the process of introducing this policy, so we may expect increasing numbers of PPI volunteers to become involved and the practice to be reported in many more types of research activity.

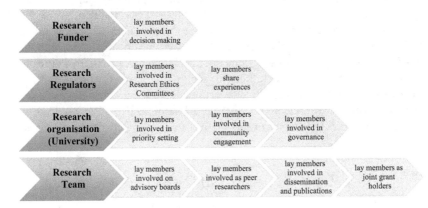

Fig. 1.1   PPI where and how

1.5   How Can PPI Increase the Power of Patients and Public to Shape Research?

Every issue we have reported on so far in this book suggests that while PPI is widely required we can identify many areas where PPI in research still needs further development if it is to be fully embedded, to work well for everyone involved and to be inclusive. For example, we have shown how great the need is for many more PPI volunteers to review research findings. Encouraging these developments in PPI in research is not a process that can happen by itself. The King's Fund in a guide proposing that researchers should work with patients as partners suggests some key components:

- *'Find collaborative partners';*
- *'Invest in developing leadership and collaborative relationships';*
- *'Make time for learning and share it';*
- *'Go where the energy is (under the radar)' and*
- *'embed collaborative activity (authorise it, make it legitimate)'. (Seale 2016)*

Nonetheless, such guidance seems to place the responsibility firmly with those organising PPI. In this book, by contrast, we are suggesting that power needs to be shared with PPI volunteers, and furthermore, that PPI volunteers may need to take power where their involvement is not adequate. We argue that effective collaboration also depends on working with those who are actively seeking such power, even if, or especially if, this is disruptive. This does not mean such involvement is automatically representative but we really do need to seek ways to think more broadly if we are going to include very diverse groups in research whose experience may be distinctly different from what we are familiar with. We will look at the concepts of inclusion and exclusion in the following chapters to address this concept.

1.6   Summary and Conclusions

For us, 'Patient and Public Involvement in research' means people from various backgrounds working together in research projects and research organisations, showing mutual respect, to make a difference by ensuring that appropriate knowledge and experience are drawn on inclusively to develop topics and evidence. It is therefore a way of working, not just a description of types of members, based on some people's views of 'us and them'. PPI can be initiated by anyone and should not be run exclusively by one section of the wider group of people involved in research.

REFERENCES

Beresford, P. (2003). *It's our lives: A short theory of knowledge, distance and experience*. London: Shaping Our Lives.

Data Protection Act. (2018). Chapter 12. TSO (The Stationary Office).

Ellis Paine, A., Hill, M., & Rochester, C. (2010). *A rose by another name: Revisiting the question: 'What exactly is volunteering'?* London: Institute for Volunteering Research.

Health and Social Care Act. (2012). Chapter 7. TSO (The Stationary Office).

Health Research Authority. (2017a). *UK policy framework for health and social care research v3.3 07/11/17*. London: Health Research Authority.

Health Research Authority. (2017b). *Health Research Authority annual report and accounts for the year to 31 March 2017*. London: NHS Health Research Authority.

Health Research Authority. (2019). *Health Research Authority annual report and accounts 2018/19*. London: NHS Health Research Authority.

Healthwatch. (2017). *Healthwatch England annual report 2016–17*. Healthwatch England.

National Institute for Health Research. (2016). *NIHR annual report 2015/16*. National Institute for Health Research.

NHS. (2015). *The NHS constitution*. London: Department of Health.

NHS England. (2017a). *Working with our patient and public voice (PPV) partners – Reimbursing expenses and paying involvement payments (v2)*. Redditch: NHS England.

NHS England. (2017b). *Patient and public participation policy*. Redditch: NHS England.

NHS England. (2017c). *Recruiting and managing volunteers in NHS providers, a practical guide*. Redditch: NHS England.

NIHR. (2018). *National standards for public involvement in research V1 March 2018*. London: NIHR.

NIHR INVOLVE (2012) Briefing notes for researchers: Public involvement in NHS, public health and social care research. Eastleigh: INVOLVE.

NIHR RDS. (approx 2014). *Patient and public involvement in health and social care research: A handbook for researchers*. London: NIHR RDS.

Price, A., Schroter, S., & Snow, R. (2018). Frequency of reporting on patient and public involvement (PPI) in research studies published in a general medical journal: A descriptive study. *BMJ Open, 8*, e020452.

Seale, B. (2016). *Patients as partners: Building collaborative relationships among professionals, patients, carers and communities*. London: King's Fund.

Simmons, P., Hawley, C., Gale, T., & Sivakumaran, T. (2010). Service user, patient, client, user or survivor: Describing recipients of mental health services. *The Psychiatrist, 34*(1), 20–23.

CHAPTER 2

Historical and Conceptual Background of Public Involvement

The relationship between the public and providers of health services and research has been transformed over two centuries by the efforts of many concerned groups.

> *Religious and charitable organisations such as Metropolitan Hospital Sunday Fund worked tirelessly not only to improve the conditions of the poor but also to place pressure on the government and local authorities to take greater responsibility for the health and welfare of London's poorest citizens. Working closely together they initiated and funded projects that gradually improved the life of all those living in London's poorest areas.* (Cook 2014)

Cook's (2014) reflective commentary on London, UK, highlights how, even 200 years ago, many people and organisations in various countries were already joining forces to campaign for access to health services for poorer people and to set up projects to change priorities for action on health. Such accounts give us valuable reminders that bringing about such changes demanded close collaboration and public debates between different groups of patient and public advocates, including famous figures like the author Charles Dickens, with government and professional organisations. While involvement in collaboration and debates has continued over the decades that followed, what health topics were debated and who joined or opposed collaborations to act on them have shifted for many reasons.

J. Grotz et al., *Patient and Public Involvement in Health and Social Care Research*, https://doi.org/10.1007/978-3-030-55289-3_2

This means that the concept of patient and public involvement (PPI) has never stood still, let alone been fixed in nature. Its dynamic character can be seen in both its history and how people think about it and use it to take action today. The constantly changing landscape of health and social care is replicated by matching shifts in the key components of PPI; different resources have come to be relevant and to be available to people, and people have had more or less power to make decisions and take social action. Patient and public involvement in the nineteenth century was linked to the efforts and moral and scientific enterprise of individuals, and public pressures and concerns forcing institutional change. In the twenty-first century, PPI has developed into a public role recognised in legislation and reflected in designated roles in organisations, and national and local government programmes. We will see the effects of these shifts in ideas and their relevance to actions appearing in every chapter in this book.

Until the nineteenth century, the relationship between people in health-related occupations and, later, health professionals and people with illnesses was very direct. If you were ill, you found someone who could help and, if you could pay, you paid them to help you. If you could not pay but one of the few church- or religious-based institutions was nearby, they might offer somewhere you might find help. This would often depend on whether you were considered to have a right to such help, perhaps through your family or community connections; because you were seen as belonging to a relevant, identified place or group; or because you could be seen as morally deserving of such help. The morally deserving might include soldiers who had been injured while serving their country; or widows who had become destitute through no fault of their own, reflected in the early foundation of charities such as widows' and orphans' funds. The Pensions Archive Trust holds records going back to 1765 when the Claimants' Widows Funds were supporting the widows and orphans of clergy in the English county of Middlesex and there are other examples of similar funds. That of the London Fire Brigade was run as a club and required members to pay regular contributions in return for benefits, including for widows and orphans. Yet others, such as the Corporation of London's Poor Widows of Freemen Fund, were, at least initially, intended to help people of high status. These funds continued into the mid-twentieth century with records for the London Fire Brigade as late as 1980.

Then in the nineteenth century, because so many people were moving to work in towns and cities where they could not call on family or community ties and could not afford to pay, new institutions came into being to support the health and welfare of large populations who needed new ways of accessing such services. These new institutions originated in different areas of society, some were voluntary, some state-provided, some religious and some secular, but all provided ways for sick people to be looked after by paid staff who had been trained in medicine, health sciences or health care.

Case Example 1   Alms Houses
Alms houses, which date back to medieval times when they were set up by religious orders, came to the fore in the Georgian and Victorian periods when they were endowed by wealthy philanthropists to mitigate the huge social problems resulting from the migration from the countryside. Their aims were to provide accommodation to allow needy elderly people to live independently but in safety and security. These continue to exist, particularly in older cities in the UK. Two continue to exist in the city of Norwich in the east of England: the Great Hospital, founded by a bishop in 1247, and Doughty's set up in 1687 to provide shelter, food and water to destitute people. Both have similar criteria to become a resident: people must have limited funds and savings, and they must have lived in the city for many years. Both are now run as charities and provide some care and support for their residents.

Alongside these, friendly societies such as The Oddfellows emerged to act as a form of health insurance with new groups of people working together to pay in to build the funds to support each other and the institutions that would provide and regulate the services. In 1875 their existence was formalised when legislation required them to be audited and registered. This recognised the contribution not only of organisations such as 'Particular Trade Societies' which were often male-dominated but also of 'Societies of Females' (Beveridge and Wells 1949: 25). Similarly, responding to urban change, in New York, in the US, in 1866 a state health department and local health boards were set up. In France, public health theorists, epidemiologists and microbiologists such as Louis Pasteur helped develop knowledge and institutions to combat communicable diseases.

The single most important overarching change in the organisation and resourcing of health care provision in the UK, was the introduction of the state National Health Service, the NHS, which is free for all citizens at the point of delivery, alongside national insurance arrangements. It also triggered a genuine paradigm shift for patient and public involvement as of right. However, after twenty years of such a state-centralised system, the decades following the 1960s saw challenges to the way the new system worked to define needs and prioritise actions. Initially, this arose from a Disability Rights Movement of activists and academics such as Judith Heumann in the US and Jane Campbell and Mike Oliver in the UK which was calling into question the involvement of 'non-disabled experts' to speak for them, and their medical interpretations of needs and actions (Barnes and Mercer 2004).

To help understand that PPI is neither a simple nor a static concept, we can start by looking back to prepare ourselves to then look to potential future developments.

In this chapter, we will look specifically at:

- The time before the NHS—when people's access to health services often depended on individual resources and variable connections to varying health institutions and organisations of health professionals.
- The changes brought by the NHS from 1948—when people's access to health support in the UK changed to depend on state organisation of resources, access and health professional education and workplaces.
- The decades following the establishment of the NHS in the UK— when health professionals consolidated their power to take decisions, but also had to recognise more complex health needs, and when private providers made inroads into service provision.
- Twenty-first-century health service changes—aiming to embed PPI in health and social care, and research.

In each case, we will consider what resources were seen as relevant, how far they were made available to people and how this affected the relative power of different groups to make decisions and take social actions to shape health-related arrangements.

2.1   Before the UK's NHS

Abel-Smith's (1964) compelling narrative shows UK hospitals between 1800 and 1948 transforming from institutions which provided limited access to people with limited health benefits, even when admitted. He estimated that in 1800 there were about 3000 patients in hospitals where the treatment provided was mostly ineffective and often actually harmful, not least because of cross-infection.

Over the 150 years after 1800, a combination of political, cultural and economic pressures encouraged a real increase in hospital capacity and in the quality of treatment provided. These were based on scientific, statistical and medical advances; the need to develop new arrangements to support major movements in populations from traditional rural communities to live and work in urban environments; changes in the training of health professionals; and in relationships between patients, health professionals and the public, the start of patient and public involvement. Public demands brought more expectations that professional status should rest on demonstrated ability to act well, accountably and for the wider good. While in 1800 there was about one bed to 5000 people, by 1961, with the NHS well-established, this had risen nearly 300-fold to about one bed for every 175 persons.

In 1800 training for doctors was moving from trade and local guilds, such as the Company of Barber-Surgeons, and the London Livery Company that trained and examined its members within the City of London, to a standardised system based on examinations and hospital experience agreed between English, Edinburgh and Dublin colleges. This reflected wider scientific, educational and professional requirements for professional training to be based on a more systematic, objective body of disciplinary knowledge determined by the Colleges of Surgeons. State registration of medics began in 1858 and, almost immediately, was suggested for the newer profession of nursing, but this was opposed by Florence Nightingale, who did not agree with any form of regulation for nursing. Disagreements continued about how nursing should be regulated and there was no state registration until after the First World War with the Nurses Regulation Act of 1919. However, several systems of training developed for nurses who, by the early twentieth century, comprised a workforce of over 70,000 in institutions, but mostly in people's homes. These were mostly women, with male nurses largely dealing with mental health care. At this time, hospitals were mostly voluntary organisations, where the nursing workforce was usually led by a matron, a chief nurse, with responsibilities for reporting directly to the hospital management committee on the nursing workforce.

These hospitals were funded by a variable mix of philanthropy, charitable giving, payments by patients and subscriptions. They were usually governed by non-medical, lay, people, mostly with a high social standing, from the aristocracy, the clergy or other religious community leaders, the emerging rich industrialists and business people and also emerging professional groups including educators and scientists. This was a starting point for patient and public involvement in decision-making. During the same period, another influential professional group, administrators, came to have increasing power, further altering and intervening in the relationship between health professionals and those affected by their clinical activities. Over this period, health was coming to be seen as an issue of public concern for community wellbeing, and a person's social status could be confirmed by being seen to help govern and administer institutions to provide health to the 'sick poor' (Rivett 2020).

Most people's access to health depended on their individual resources and their often precarious connections to varying health institutions, and members of organisations of health professionals. During the nineteenth century, two developments became more marked, affecting people's access to hospital care: the appearance of diverse types of 'medically specialist' hospitals as opposed to generalist hospitals; and the increasing emphasis on 'cure' rather than 'care'. On the one hand, the ability of health professionals to cure grew. On the other, as voluntary organisations, hospitals were dependent on their funding sources with their specific interests. As their fundraisers became able to demonstrate 'successful results', many became reluctant to admit types of case they could not cure with more general facilities and skills. Many hospitals, particularly in large urban centres, were founded to ensure specialist care could be provided for a specific illness which could not served by general hospitals and where medical specialists could build their skills and apply them. To gain treatment in these hospitals, therefore, potential patients might have to provide satisfactory evidence, perhaps to one of the increasingly powerful administrators of the specialist hospital, that they had the only condition the specialist hospital would treat. So poor patients then found themselves having to demonstrate that they were 'a deserving case' either on moral or medical grounds.

While community health might be of growing public concern, not everyone had the same rights to access or to shape the institutions that were developing to deal with those concerns. In this context, we need to consider the state of social policy at that time. Earlier in the nineteenth century, an individual's money and social influence was the most likely factor to determine whether they could gain access to health care resources and institutions, by literally buying them outright if they were very rich, or buying some access through subscriptions or associations.

If they had no money, they would be subject to a haphazard, and even corrupt, system of seeking external 'relief', exemplified by the Poor Laws and the workhouses, and reflected in the UK's colonies and dominions such as parts of Canada. Here gatekeepers could demand unofficial payments from applicants with no firm guarantees of receiving any health or social care; and if the applicants were completely lacking money, they were heavily dependent on the judgements of powerful others as to whether they were considered morally or medically 'deserving'. In the UK and Germany, the formal decisions about who was deserving or eligible as a 'medically-specialist or curable case' were initially made by the governing bodies of the hospitals, but with growing numbers of patients these were increasingly made by a newly emerging group of administrators whose role changed over time from being governors and gate-keeping almoners to become members of the paid profession of social worker.

Exercise 2.1
In what ways did lay people have a say in how hospitals were organised in the nineteenth and early twentieth century, before 1940s state health provision like the NHS? What resources helped different groups of lay people have a say at that time?

In a parallel process, those with moderate means were seen to organise themselves to fund their own health and social care in Friendly or Mutual Aid Societies which were found across Europe from the eighteenth century onwards. William Beveridge (1948) acknowledged their role, and relevance, in the context of considering whether establishing the NHS might become feasible and acceptable. He also envisaged how building on their role might pose tensions for the political, social and medical groups in power both in the medical institutions and in the wider society:

WHEN, in the last years of the eighteenth century, the aristocratic rulers of Britain began to concern themselves with friendly societies, they were torn between conflicting desires. On the one hand, they wanted working-men to get together, to make provision against the calamities of sickness, death and old age; only if the "industrious classes" did more to provide for themselves could the burden to provide for them under the Poor Law be lightened for other classes. On the other hand, with the French Revolution in full view, there appeared to the then rulers of Britain to be the obvious dangers in causing the industrious classes to get together too much; there was fear that they might get together to change the constitution. (Beveridge 1948: 63)

Beveridge suggests here that this might be seen as saving resources for the wider and more advantaged sections of society, who would otherwise have to pay taxes to support the Poor Law, if working people collectively provided for themselves. However, he goes on to argue that strengthening their experience of acting collectively might put working people in a stronger position to act to change the structure of political governance as well as health governance. Neither the political ruling classes nor the medical establishment would necessarily and easily give up the power they had held up till then. This is an important lesson for patient and public involvement. If ordinary people are allowed to express their needs and views on the services they use, the power of medical practitioners and administrators must, to some extent, be reduced.

Important for what happened next were characteristically British cultural practices through which people had traditionally organised themselves with others to deliver some social care in a particularly British way. Bourdillon (1945), writing before the birth of the welfare state to document existing 'Voluntary Social Services' in Britain, describes the usual process for transforming an impulse for voluntary action into setting up a voluntary society.

The habit of forming voluntary associations for every sort of social purpose is widely spread and deeply rooted in this country. Quite naturally in Britain when a man has a new enthusiasm he buys a two penny notebook, prints 'Minute Book' carefully in the first page, calls together some of his friends under the name of a Committee – and behold a new voluntary society is launched. (Bourdillon 1945: 1)

The extent to which the idea and practice of organising such voluntary social services was embedded in ordinary community life at that time was confirmed by its routinely taking place in local pubs, as Beveridge and Wells (1949) demonstrate from evidence in Mass Observation reports.

> *The Slate Club, The Help-out Club (a women's Holiday and Christmas Club), Cricket and Football Clubs, the Rambler' Club, the Darts Club, and the Horticultural Society are among the varied groups organised from the Unicorn [the local pub].* (Beveridge and Wells 1949: 27)

Thus in the 1940s, we find several groups with varying levels of power and influence in health and social care services: health professionals; governing bodies of lay people usually of high social status; patients; administrators and people organising themselves, either to cover medical expenses when in need or as mutual aid initiatives. By and large, the patients at that time constituted the stakeholder group holding the least power. Overall, before the NHS was set up, access to treatment and patient and public involvement in shaping what was seen as important, and in overseeing its delivery as accessible and acceptable, were largely dependent on social standing, money, 'medical interest' and the ability and means to organise mutual aid. However, all of these groups can be seen as playing important parts in enabling what came to be established as a National Health Service.

Key Questions 2.1
What new opportunities for involvement were becoming available between the world wars?
What new opportunities for involvement do you see becoming available?

2.2   NATIONAL HEALTH SERVICES CHANGES IN 1948

The introduction of the NHS, putting UK health services into public ownership, removed overnight many inequitable restrictions on people's access to health services. Yet, in doing so, it also removed most direct patient and public involvement altogether. Now patients could expect to receive health care irrespective of whether or not they had money and whether or not privileged people deemed them to be deserving. Poorer people could also expect to get free social care although from the beginning this was means-tested so that better-off people could expect to have to pay for at least some of their social care.

However, public ownership did not translate into public control, except when people voted at the ballot box for parties with particular health and welfare policies. New laws introduced at this time, notably the National Health Services Act 1946 and the Nurses Act 1949, established a comprehensive system of control by the state, in place of the previous wide variety of forms of involvement by different groups. These included lay groups linked, for instance, to religious communities, charitable associations, bereaved families, injured service personnel or friendly societies. The new NHS arrangements did away with the lay governance of hospitals and ended the power of mutual aid friendly societies. It was also argued that there would be much less need for the voluntary social services as the welfare state would take over most social care responsibilities in a similar way to the NHS covering health.

In setting up the welfare state, particularly the NHS, Beveridge (1948) again summed up its profound consequences for patient and public involvement, for example through friendly societies. He suggested that they could turn their attention to more general, less health-specific charitable activities. He recognised the vitality of the community spirit that such collective activities could stimulate and channel and that it was important not to waste such community-based energies.

> *The hospital contributory schemes, like the friendly societies, are profoundly affected by the effects of State action. Their amazing recent developments have shown the driving force that emerges when local feeling can be combined with Mutual Aid. It would be disastrous if the spirit that has gone to building up these associations should now be lost. They may continue for special medical treatment. What one would like to see would be that they should explore the possibility of applying their methods to benevolent purposes generally.* (ibid: 292)

Beveridge's concerns were borne out by how little support the welfare state gave to making community and public involvement integral to shaping the new arrangements.

At the same time, the medical professionals, who had held much of the operational control before the establishment of the NHS, lost most of it, despite having put up considerable active resistance to the new arrangements. Similarly, the role of administrators shifted from deciding who received treatment, fundraising and making the case for services to be funded to making decisions instead on how such treatment would be delivered and how it would be rationed in some circumstances. This is not to say that one system was in every way better than the other, or that the changes were wholly standardised and wholly consistent with a new and different set of values, laws and policies, as many nuances in practices and approaches developed over time. However, the NHS undeniably brought in changes that were fundamental and dramatic.

> *the voluntary hospitals were nationalised and managed by unelected Regional Hospital Boards (RHBs) alongside ex-local government institutions, while GPs were administered separately and local authorities were left with residual pub-lic health and social care functions.* (Gorsky 2008: 442)

Exercise 2.2
What reasons might doctors have had for resisting the NHS being set up?
What reasons might doctors have had to see advantages in the new NHS?
What reasons might patients and members of the public have had for seeking to be actively involved in the new NHS?

Bevan, in his own words, 'stuffed the mouths of the doctors with gold', guaranteeing them a system of rewards for carrying out education and being responsible for delivering but not owning specified areas of health care. This narrowed their remaining scope for exercising power to taking actions to assert the superiority of their professional knowledge over that of policymakers and administrators, and of course the public recipients of the system.

2.3   Diversifying Health Services

Until the late twentieth century, health professionals consolidated their power to take decisions and organise resources, but also had to recognise the complex needs of more groups, with some people's needs increasingly being met through private providers, and lay members becoming appointed as non-executive directors on hospital boards and elected to their governing bodies.

The health services changes of the late 1940s appeared to dismiss the idea that public and patient groups had anything useful or legitimate to contribute to the organisation of health services. Medical professionals and bio-scientists argued for the view that clinical needs should be used to govern how health provision should be developed and who should have access to it. However, at least some of these changes were being reversed from the 1960s onwards when other political, policy, organisational and community developments raised new issues which called into question the idea that only a small number of groups should have the right to exercise power to shape health services and evidence. Instead, other groups such as the Disability Alliance were putting the view that power might need to be distributed amongst a variety of stakeholders whose voices might need to be heard and different types of knowledge acknowledged. These included patient and disability support groups, such as those working with people living with cerebral palsy, or deaf communities whose members came to expect to play a much more visible range of public roles, increasingly as leaders and researchers as well as employees.

In 1974, Barbara Castle, then the Labour Minister of Health, introduced community health councils (CHCs), calling for them to be developed into 'a powerful forum where consumer views can influence the NHS and the local participation in the running of the NHS can become reality'. CHCs operated on the same areas as local health authorities, covering all local services. They introduced patient complaint and advocacy systems, participated in the development of new services and campaigned against 'irresponsible' plans to close hospitals, wards and beds. They continued until the end of 2002 when they were replaced in turn by patient and public involvement forums, local involvement networks and finally local Healthwatch organisations, which remain in existence.

Doctors acted to consolidate their power after the NHS was established (Rudolf Klein 2010) as various responses to the NHS being created, then reinvented, demonstrate. Perhaps surprisingly, doctors moved from being very vocal opponents of the NHS to become its strongest supporters, as they found they could reassert their professional power.

Above all, the medical profession had made sure the governments, whatever their ideology or ambition, would think long and hard before seeking to change the structure of the NHS in any way which would bring the underlying concordat with the medical profession into question: from being the main opponents of the NHS, the doctors had in effect become the strongest force for the status quo.
(Klein 2010: 42)

Salter (2015) argues that changes such as the introduction of waiting lists increased the power of the medical professional to regulate the delivery of health services by rationing to enable their organisations to meet or manage health targets.

The status quo at that time meant that patients and the public had no voice. Since then, however, various groups have increasingly found ways to resist being co-opted to work within health organisations, yet still silenced and being excluded. A range of service user and community groups, ethnic minorities and other groups asserting cultural and other distinctive needs have become more vocal, articulating the view that power did not seem to have shifted in any way to reflect the growing recognition of complex needs and diversity in the wider society as populations, expectations, family structures and cultures changed. For example, the National Survivor User Network (NSUN) was set up early in the twenty-first century 'to build a more united and confident mental health service user movement' and was based on user-led research led by service users, coordinated by Jan Wallcraft, which resulted in the report 'On Our Own Terms' in 2003. In 2013 they launched 4Pi national involvement standards.

Disability activists were a notable voice of dissent in the face of medical power, bringing pressures for change in health institutions and their relationships with the people they served.

> *Disabled activists became increasingly discontented with 'pressure group' activity as a means of achieving social change. A further grievance was the 'colonisation' of disability organisations by non disabled 'experts'. Such concerns encouraged moves towards a 'grassroots' politics, with organisations controlled by disabled people.* (Barnes and Mercer 2004: 1)

Activists like Campbell argued that 'professionals, experts and others who seek to help must be committed to promoting such control by disabled people' (Campbell 2001).

The monopoly of the NHS was challenged in different ways as, following the election of a conservative government led by Margaret Thatcher in 1979, the government sought numerous ways to introduce markets across many service areas that had previously been exclusively public-run, including health. This dramatically altered the landscape of principles, institutions and resources, and in turn how services should be delivered in practice. This was seen in a series of health policy changes in the late 1980s which held organisations' managers more accountable for implementing policy; increased competitive tendering; subsidised contributions to private insurance and notably strengthened patients' rights through patient charters. The 1990 NHS and Community Care Act introduced an internal market in which suppliers of health services competed; GPs' powers increased in comparison to hospital doctors; and health status improvement targets were introduced. As a result of this legislation, from 1991 onwards lay people were appointed as non-executive directors to hospital and other NHS trust boards. These were defined as people who were not employed by the trust; they held, or had held, senior positions in health services, local government, industry and the voluntary and charity sector, echoing the situation in the nineteenth century. *"Taken together, the reforms have increased the influence of market forces in making allocative decisions"* (Allsop 1995: 12).

Introducing accountability for how policies were implemented and referring to market principles suggested that patients might also have consumer rights to quality and choice, which in turn suggested they might have further rights to information and to review performance. Allsop mentions how patient charters were reviewed by the director of the King's Fund in 1991 in a letter to the British Medical Journal. This raised explicit and related criticisms, specifically calling attention to a wide range of groups being excluded from services, the information they needed to support choices and knowledge of standards of appropriate access and treatment.

Since the 1970s, commentators on health inequalities from Black (Department of Health and Social Security 1980) to Marmot (2010) have repeatedly underlined the persistent advantages that those classes with higher incomes, education, connections and status have in gaining better access to "free" resources such as health services, leading to clearly better health chances.

Some more serious charges may be levelled at the charter in its current form. The first is that it is something of a middle class charter: standards for waiting times and so on are important only if you already have reasonable access to health care. For a substantial number of people from ethnic minorities or with disabilities or who are homeless the charter may seem irrelevant. Despite the emphasis on information nothing in the charter suggests that patients should have a right to written information in a language they understand and personal communication through interpreters if necessary. Respect for religions and cultural beliefs is included, but not the right of women to be examined by another woman in sensitive specialties such as obstetrics and gynaecology. The other concern is the omission of anything on standards of clinical care, which seems odd given that this is what the NHS is about and that what people want, above all, is the most effective treatment for their condition. Patients would like a guarantee that standards are being monitored and poor performance is being weeded out. (Stocking 1991: 1149)

Looking at those criticisms made in the 1990s, we can see that in the last thirty years we have greatly increased awareness of the diverse ways in which different groups can be systematically excluded from access to health services and from informing and deciding on service changes and the evidence-building needed to address these. What is less clear is what progress has been made in embedding PPI to help make these changes in practice.

Exercise 2.3
Where did pressure come from to reintroduce patient and public involvement?
What new resources helped different groups of lay people to have a say since the 1970s?

2.4   TWENTY-FIRST-CENTURY CHANGES: EMBEDDING PPI IN HEALTH AND SOCIAL CARE AND RESEARCH

Following the UK general election in 1997, a New Labour government, keen to reduce health inequalities, introduced sweeping reforms in the running of the NHS with a new regime of extensive target-based planning and evaluation. Policy at the time was influenced by Giddens (1998) and 'The Third Way', intending to bring about a renewal of social democracy. In 2001 the Department of Health published a White Paper, 'Shifting the Balance of Power within the NHS', which suggested that involving patients and the public should become embedded in the workings of the NHS to balance service reforms which were driven from Whitehall.

The NHS Plan sets out our ambitions to create a patient centred NHS. Our vision is to move away from an outdated system, towards a new model where the voice of the patient is heard through every level of the service, acting as a powerful lever for change and improvement. Our goal is to move away from a paternalistic model of decision making, towards a model of partnership, whereby citizens have a greater connection with their local services, and have a say in how they are designed, developed and delivered. (Department of Health 2001: 26)

In 2006 Pat Gay published findings from a study by the Institute for Volunteering Research which described some of the objections to such an approach:

To begin with, many senior managers had seen lay participation as an unwelcome challenge to their authority, and had some anxieties about their work being held up to scrutiny by people who might not have the understanding to make constructive comments. In addition, they felt irritation at the extra time they would have to spend in explanations and justifications. The culture and philosophy underlying professional practice could act as an overall barrier to involvement. (Gay 2006: 88)

However, such objections were overcome and many of the changes outlined in 2001 were later enshrined in law, most notably in 2012, as flagged up in Chap. 1. While the organisation of the NHS changed from a central system to a multiplicity of diverse trusts and private facilities, more public voices were heard, as elected governors of NHS trusts and in patient participation groups for GP surgeries. While some might challenge the proportion of governors who are retired health professionals and while members of patient participation groups are mainly white, middle class and older people, they nonetheless represent a step in the direction of change towards more involvement. Publicly funded but independent organisations such as local Healthwatch organisations run by boards of trustees are now playing the role of consumer champions highlighting the health quality needs of many often-excluded groups in the community such as the homeless, offenders, people with mental health problems, looked after children, people with dementia and carers. As we will see in Chap. 5, this is not the end of a period of development lasting more than a century.

2.5   Summary and Conclusions

We set out to show how the concept of patient and public involvement is not static and that its key components, resources, power and social action, have moved constantly over the last few centuries. The current model of PPI can therefore not only be traced back to the 1960s as a public response to a failure by policymakers, health service organisations and research communities to include the views of patients and the public (Wilson et al. 2015) but should be seen as a process with much earlier origins that continues today.

This process has important implications for individuals planning PPI in a changing NHS in the future. Private providers and public providers of both services and research may seek to involve patients and the public in very different ways.

The process of patients, members of the public and perhaps some policymakers using patient and public involvement as a means of changing the distribution of power is at best still in its infancy. From recent changes in welfare and disability payments to funding for research, the experience of those in control of the process, the medical profession and administrators, has become increasingly divergent from the experience and aspirations of those affected by the decisions and those seeking to be involved, and who, paradoxically, are currently excluded. (see Beresford 2016).

Patient and public involvement in health and social care, and evidencing health and social care, is therefore neither a fixed state nor an abstract aspiration. It is about people taking up opportunities to exercise power and rights, to influence decisions on and to ensure they have equitable rights of access to health and social care. Learning from the history of people's involvement in health and social care over the last two centuries, we can see how resources and opportunities for involvement constantly change as the wider society, public expectations, health and social care institutions and knowledge constantly develop and adapt. Our political systems are underpinned by the sharing of power which may not be easily shared. We nonetheless argue that different groups should exercise their differing means of accessing power to advance important value-based goals such as equitable ability to shape decisions. In the case of PPI in health and social care, this has meant looking critically at the developing power of both the medical profession and the administrators involved in allocating resources to services and research, in comparison to the power of those patients and members of the public who will be most directly affected by decisions to allocate resources, time and space.

Before the NHS was set up in the UK in 1948, determining and reviewing rights to health and social care resources and, to some extent, shared decision-making, power over access to such resources was more directly and openly based on higher social status and economic advantages, which effectively excluded those with no or few such means. The NHS transformed this imbalance by guaranteeing wider social access to resources, but also centralised control with members of the medical profession and government departments. Paradoxically this actually limited the ability of the public and service users to exercise their voice and expertise in shaping provision and research. Since then, slowly but progressively, diverse patient and public voices have re-entered these processes. Now, at a time when uncertainties are many and multiplying in relation to public and private funding, alongside the introduction of many new ways of organising health and social care services and research, we cannot predict what directions involvement will take. However, we can learn from the dynamic history of PPI, which shows us that to promote effective public and patient involvement it is of prime importance to actively identify opportunities as they emerge and to argue for the relevance of public involvement in decision-making in health and social care.

At an international, despite many positive developments in each continent and despite active global encouragement from lead organisations such as the World Health Organisation, many countries are still having to begin finding their way to develop such involvement. Troya, Bartlam and Chew-Graham (2018) have identified how many mental health support groups have strenuously argued the case for public involvement in mental health research in Latin America. But they have commented that despite governments in Chile and Ecuador having developed policies and legislation to encourage this, political and financial constraints have meant public involvement in the continent is still 'under-developed'. Nonetheless, Caxaj et al. (2014) have reported impressive community involvement in research on mental health problems in Guatemalan communities affected by mining exploitation. Here, the community co-designed all research processes from data collection via group interviews and participatory action research to select research participants and share in data analysis, respecting their shared histories. We may therefore need to find new ways to use each other's histories to listen, learn and encourage more widely inclusive involvement in each other's countries.

However, Professor Peter Mittler has demonstrated in speaking and writing about his own experience of living with dementia and campaigning that it is possible to include the voices of people with dementia; doing this has transformed society's assumptions about who may need to be included in policy-making and decisions about support for this group internationally as well as in the UK:

> *I have published a memoir, edited a selection of my papers for publication and contributed several new papers to academic and professional journals on the implementation of the new United Nations Convention on the Rights of Persons with Disabilities which could greatly improve the quality of life and support for all disabled people, including those living with dementia.* (Mittler 2011: 146)

REFERENCES

Abel-Smith, B. (1964). *The hospitals 1800–1948.* London: Heinemann Educational Books.

Allsop, J. (1995). *Health policy and the NHS towards 2000.* London: Routledge.

Barnes, C., & Mercer, G. (Eds.). (2004). *Implementing the social model of disability: Theory and research.* Leeds: The Disability Press.

Beresford, P. (2016). *All our welfare.* Bristol: Policy Press.

Beveridge, L. (1948). *Voluntary action.* London: George Allen & Unwin.

Beveridge, L., & Wells, A. F. (1949). *The evidence for voluntary action.* London: George Allen & Unwin.

Bourdillon, A. F. C. (1945). *Voluntary social services: Their place in the modern state.* London: Methuen.

Campbell, J. (2001). Valuing diversity: The disability agenda – We've only just Begun. Independent Living Foundation, Internet publication. www.independentliving.org/docs6/campbell20011109.html

Caxaj, S., Berman, H., Varcoe, C., Ray, S. L., & Restoulec, J. P. (2014). Gold mining on Mayan-Mam territory: Social unravelling, discord and distress in the Western highlands of Guatemala. *Social Science and Medicine, 111,* 50–57.

Cook, B. (2014). *A reflection on sickness and poverty in London in the late 19th century. London Catalyst Museum of London poverty essay.* Museum of London.

Department of Health. (2001). *Shifting the balance of power within the NHS: Securing delivery.* London: Department of Health Publications.

Department of Health and Social Security. (1980). *Inequalities in health: Report of a research working group.* London: Department of Health and Social Security.

Gay, P. (2006). Participation for health. *Voluntary Action, 8*(1), 79–91.

Giddens, A. (1998). *The third way: The renewal of social democracy.* Cambridge: Polity Press.

Gorsky, M. (2008). The British National Health Service 1948–2008: A review of the historiography. *Social History of Medicine, 21*(3), 437–460.

Klein, R. (2010). *The new politics of the NHS: From creation to reinvention sixth edition.* Oxford: Radcliffe Publishing.

Marmot, M. (2010). Fair society, healthy lives: The Marmot Review. Strategic review of health inequalities in England post-2010. Publisher: The Marmot Review.

Mittler, P. (2011). Editorial: Journey into Alzheimerland. *Dementia. The International Journal of Social Research and Practice, 10*(2), 145–147.

Rivett, G. (2020). *The history of the NHS.* Available on: https://www.nuffieldtrust.org.uk/health-and-social-care-explained/the-history-of-the-nhs/

Salter, B. (2015). *The politics of change in the health service.* London: Macmillan International Education.

Stocking, B. (1991). Patient's charter: New right issue. *BMJ, 303,* 1148–1149.

Troya, M. I., Bartlam, B., & Chew-Graham, C. A. (2018). Involving the public in health research in Latin America: Making the case for mental health. *Revista Panamericana de Salud Pública, 42,* e45.

Wilson, P., et al. (2015). *ReseArch with Patient and Public invOlvement: A RealisT evaluation – The RAPPORT study.* Southampton: NIHR Journals Library.

CHAPTER 3

PPI in Research Practice

The key ideas and historical insights we brought into Chap. 2 help us understand how debates and actions have enabled more, or less, patient and public involvement (PPI) in health and social care. In this chapter, we will look at the practicalities of involving patients and the public in health and social care research which emerged from this dynamic context. While there has been a recent dramatic increase in the volume of published guidance, this offers varying amounts of detail which support very different types of activity. Some is intended to 'prompt thinking' (Nuffield Department of Primary Care Health Sciences 2015) while others set out processes for planning PPI (Jacobs et al. 2017). This book seeks to equip individuals and groups involved in health and social care research to work out for themselves the best way to develop collaborative working with patients and the public appropriate within the projects and processes on which they are about to embark.

This chapter will concentrate on building PPI into research practice and the relationships associated with this, recognising that any form of involvement must contribute not only to the quality of the research activities but also to the experience of being involved. This is essential both for ensuring that the rationale for any project can be shared and also for helping guarantee that individuals being involved will be treated with respect. We will draw on the terms explained in Chap. 1 to distinguish between participation, engagement and involvement, helping the reader to appreciate that 'involvement' in research is not the same as 'participation'. This

© The Author(s) 2020

J. Grotz et al., *Patient and Public Involvement in Health and Social Care Research*, https://doi.org/10.1007/978-3-030-55289-3_3

chapter is therefore **not** about ways to find people to take part in a study as subjects or donors of information. It is also **not** about how to design research projects using a methodology based on participation, in which lay people would be involved as peer researchers.

Instead, the main purpose of this chapter is to illustrate how patient and public involvement in research practice follows from clear principles, to understand who, when and how to involve patients and the public. 'Who' is potentially any member of society, but ideally in health and social care research it would be those who have direct experience of those issues the research aims to inform; 'when' is always best seen as happening from the very start of a study all the way through to sharing its findings; and 'how' is always about ways of working with appropriate care and respect. We will conclude this chapter by, importantly, looking at how and when things can go wrong, something the current guidance still often neglects.

We will now go on to look in more detail at:

- The principles of patient and public involvement in research
- Who to be involved with
- When to be involved
- How to be involved
- The practicalities of involvement
- What may go wrong and planning to deal with it

3.1   The Principles of Patient and Public Involvement in Research

An overriding principle in planning and organising research is that it should do no harm. All other research and involvement principles must flow from this. This is more fully addressed in Chap. 4 on Ethics. This means that neither research nor involvement can be a waste of people's time. Those planning the research must not be deceitful, falsely promising chances to influence decision-making where that is not possible. Under no circumstances should being involved leave those involved feeling or doing worse, physically or mentally. In 2018 the UK's National Institute for Health Research (NIHR) published National Standards for Public Involvement in Research. These did not explicitly refer to the basic principles we have just outlined, but they clearly drew on comparable principles. The NIHR Standards specifically state: the need for researchers to offer opportunities that are accessible; the value of collaboration; the need to provide appropriate support and use plain language; the need to understand what difference involvement makes to research; and, to quote the National Standards, to be committed *"to involve the public in our governance and leadership so that our decisions promote and protect the public interest"* (NIHR 2018: 5).

Evidence about what happens in practice suggests that achieving effective involvement which does apply these principles depends on there being good leadership within the research projects where involvement happens (Poland et al. 2019; Keenan et al. 2019). While it is noteworthy that the NIHR has published the principles, translating them into practice in a consistent manner requires the commitment of organisational and project leadership. For this reason, the second most important principle for involvement is that a research organisation needs to demonstrate transparently and explicitly how it is committed to patient and public involvement, showing what relevant policies it has in place, and what it does to support continuous improvement in its involvement practices. If a project involved patients and members of the public in research which could not demonstrate this clear commitment, this might well breach the principles of involvement. This would mean that individuals would not have been fully informed about what being involved would mean and so the project would be unethical. As we cannot assume that every organisation has included these principles in their overall practice, those setting out to organise PPI in their own research will need to closely examine their own organisation's arrangements to clarify how far these principles have been put into practice or what needs to happen to ensure that they do so.

3.2   WHO TO BE INVOLVED WITH

As we explained in Chap. 1, all kinds of people can be involved. Examples include: people with the condition a health research project is investigating; carers; people from a particular community on which the research focuses; or people with other personal or specialist insights. 'Community' in this case may relate to either a specific geographical area, members of a particular ethnic minority or faith, or people with a common interest. A key criterion for considering people as PPI members of the research team should be that the individuals concerned can contribute to the research and want to do so as volunteers willing to be involved. Nobody should be excluded because of their ability, whether physical or because of a learning disability, or because of limits set by how their contribution is organised. We will go on later to examine the types of help some people may need if they are to contribute to involvement, and how organisers will need to identify, consider and address their access needs.

Our starting point that anybody can be involved means we need to consider who should be involved in each specific case and how decisions should be taken to bring this about. In Chap. 1 we posed the question: Why may we want patient and public representatives to be involved in the project? Is it because they have direct experience of the issues being researched, so that involving them reduces the distance between their experience and understanding and the findings of research being implemented? Is it because their views can help shape the way the research is managed? An example of this is where minority communities see a topic such as blood transfusions or the treatment of the dead as taboo or governed by strict religious stipulations. Their views can help show how to present plans for or findings from research on that topic in appropriate language to engage, not alienate such communities. Is it an act of exercising democracy? Or is it required by law? Attending to all these questions can help in deciding what characteristics may be most appropriate when encouraging particular people to be involved in specific research, and in some cases the range of people needed. However, having decided who to involve, this still raises the important question about how or where to find the right people, who may want to get involved.

Table 3.1 provides a list of groups researchers or organisers may be working with, or whose members use the services covered by the research topic and who may agree to be involved as members of the public or patients.

Table 3.1 Groups to help find people to involve as members of the public or patients

Recruiters and matchers	Many research organisations fund bodies who recruit local volunteers and groups and match them with research teams. These bodies are always keen to hear from researchers and volunteers to join in this process
Previous research participants	People who have been involved in one research project as lay members or participants may be willing to be involved in different activities and roles in future research, for example by bringing insights into how to better recruit and retain research participants. They may be contacted through networks of researcher, self-help, charitable and voluntary groups
Service providers	Service providers, including hospitals, community services and GPs, often have their own patient reference groups for general services or specific conditions. If the research involves a specific service or medication, they may be able to help
Charities and voluntary organisations	Larger charities, in particular those that focus on specific conditions, often have their own support groups for services users to help with their decision-making, including decisions on research. These charities may be open to discussions and to helping to find suitable people to be involved, or the charities may be interested in becoming directly involved in locating potentially interested people
Self-help groups	People come together to support each other in self-help groups about many issues, from memory loss to mental health and from trauma to addiction. Their meetings are often restricted to members but they may be interested and willing to share a request to contact people who may want to be involved in shaping research
Carers, service users and survivors	Carers, service users and survivors have direct personal experiences. They may be reached through targeted advertising, networking, social media and direct contact, either individually or through support groups
Community representatives	Leaders of communities whether of location, faith or interest such as organisers of community groups, parish councillors, priests and leaders of ethnic minority or older people's groups are knowledgeable about who is active and interested in their communities. Even if they do not become involved themselves, they may be able to help to find people who can and want to be involved

These groups are not mutually exclusive. In most cases you will be looking for a mix of people with different lived experiences from different social and ethnic backgrounds and of different ages; one of these groups is unlikely to give you access to everybody you need. One of the accusations about groups of people involved is that they are predominantly white, middle class and older. The mix not only gives you access to the range of experience to make your knowledge and findings robust, but may also generate discussion among the lay members that will help you to refine your views.

Using recruiters and matchers or previous research participants can bring several advantages, particularly if your research is a continuation of a previous project or part of a programme. They may be able to support you, for example, with ideas on how to achieve what you want to, based on their previous experience, but also support newcomers, particularly those who lack confidence.

However, you need to be careful when accepting people who have had a lot of previous experience. Some may come to the point where they think more like researchers than lay members so that they start to have views on the right way of working and judge for themselves which of their experiences are valuable to put forward; their behaviour may also put off other lay members. The same may apply to retired health and care professionals though they may also provide invaluable insights, particularly if the way a service is delivered is returning to earlier practices.

Service providers often have their own patient reference groups but are also members of regional or national research networks. The NHS uses the number of patients put forward by organisations to be involved in research as a measure of quality. However, providers can also give direct access to patients. An organisation contributing to research on end of life care contacted current service users and the families of past service users to ask if they were prepared to get involved.

Charities and voluntary organisations vary tremendously from large national organisations that may be similar in size to large corporations to small local operations. They may focus on a specific condition, such as cancer or dementia, or communities of interest such as disabled people or older people. Some have very great influence, lobbying within their areas of interest and contributing to research at national level. They may provide information, services and support, sometimes through contracts with the health service or local authorities. They may also receive funding from commercial businesses, including, for example, pharmaceutical companies, and this may cause some academics to question their independence. Similarly, some members of the public with an interest in a specific research topic may question the validity of paid staff speaking on behalf of those with lived experience. Both these concerns are discussed in Chap. 6. However, many charities and voluntary organisations have local branches throughout the country which may provide direct access to patients and members of the public. Voluntary organisations may also be an appropriate source of suitable people in communities.

Self-help groups differ from charities and voluntary organisations in that they tend to be local. Those supporting people with specific medical conditions and their carers may be supported by or linked to hospitals or a large national charity. Others, including those aimed at people with dementia, carers or older people, have been set up by volunteers to meet a need in their community. They may receive funding from the organisation that supports them or under a programme run by their local authority, but the sums involved tend to be small and often relate to specific activities, so they need also to raise funds themselves. These groups may be a good way of reaching directly a wide range of people who have, or have recovered from, specific conditions and their carers, or particular sectors of the population without having to resort to wider media. They are also helpful when working with communities in that they can take you to the grassroots.

As Table 3.1 suggests, seeking contacts in the community requires time and persistence.

It may occasionally be appropriate to make honorary appointments. For example, if research is high profile or of interest to the public, the research group may wish to invite a senior academic or a person well known in the area covered by the research topic to chair the board. Similarly, if the project requires a lot of communications with patients and members of the public, the project board may wish to appoint somebody in addition to the usual communications staff to ensure that these are appropriate.

The term stakeholder is widely used in connection with research but, like involvement, engagement and participation, it has a range of interpretations. It can mean anything from the patients and the public involved in a research project; through everyone directly involved in the work of a project; to everyone who has a link to the project, including service providers and users, commissioners, research funders and many others. It is important to determine how the term is being used; the broader definition may actually exclude patients and the public from involvement because the research leaders regard communication with the wider group as adequate.

3.3   When to Be Involved

The simple answer to the question of when to involve people is ideally to start from the very beginning of the research activity. However, ideas for research come from many sources: a new idea from an individual; following on from existing research; meeting an identified need or solving a specific problem; being part of a wider university or health and care programme;

responding to a call for proposals from a funding body; or as a result of existing patient and public involvement work by a charity or voluntary organisation. It may not, therefore, be easy to work out when a research project actually begins without identifying where the research is coming from.

Exercise 3.1
Consider the question: When does a research project begin if researchers are bringing together a team to respond to a call for research proposals from a funding body?

One approach for people to organise or become involved in research is to base their decisions on a diagram of the research cycle (see example in Fig. 3.1) using it as a starting point to help them to identify when and how to involve patients and the public (see, e.g. Turk et al. 2017; NIHR INVOLVE 2012). This shows planning as a process following logically from first having an idea through planning, seeking and gaining funding, then carrying out the various stages of a project, to disseminating and evaluating its findings. This evaluation may lead in turn to a new idea and to starting the cycle again.

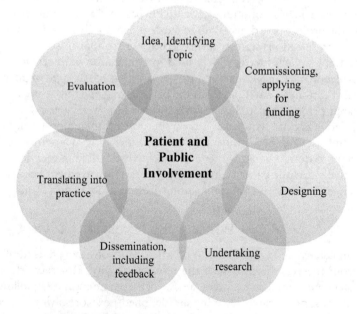

Fig. 3.1 Patient and public involvement at the centre of the research cycle

A problem with this approach is that it is too linear. It takes the idea or topic as a starting point, but does not put it into context. Taking context into account means working out: whether the origins of the idea mean that it is starting from scratch or not; if it is part of a programme or to gain funding, what criteria will the project need to meet; or whether a lot of information is already available, perhaps from earlier research. Even if any of these applies, the focus and scope of the project will still need to be defined or refined; involving patients and the public may contribute to this. PPI participants bring lived experience of taking medication, receiving treatment, using services or supporting people who do any of these. They often have access to a wider community with similar experiences on which they can draw. The researchers may well come to the project with a different knowledge, perhaps the technical details of a medicine or procedure, or specifications describing how the service should be delivered.

Different people need to collaborate to optimise the focus and scope of research. However, the first moves will most likely be decided by the research lead, and any members of their team, or an organisation commissioning the research. In the first instance, those involved need to review what information they have available to them already and identify gaps in their knowledge; what more they need to be clear about how to move forward; and who they need to talk to in order to learn about lived experience. They also need to be sure that everyone agrees on the rationale for the project and has the same understanding about the research topic. This will help the researcher to identify where to look for help in identifying patients and members of the public whose experience can be relevant, and how to involve them in the first instance. It is important to remember that being involved will include not only patients and the public but also people who work in the area for which the research is planned. The balance between the three groups, researchers service providers and the public, will depend on the nature of the research. As soon as people from different backgrounds become involved, however, the researchers need to start to build relationships of trust and respect.

A short conversation can help identify a focus, or it can be done through a simple survey or a focus group to discuss patients' or carers' experiences. Yet even here it is advisable to involve a small number of patients in preparing the survey, using their experience as a basis to ensure that all the key areas have been covered, and also that the approach is accessible for the target audience. We discuss the practicalities of access in Sect. 3.5. In some cases, it may be necessary to bring in more specialist knowledge may be needed at this stage, particularly if the project includes a technical aspect. Whichever approach is used, the number of people involved and the discussions or questions need to be limited to producing the information required. The preparatory stage may be an iterative process; you may not get all the answers you need first time, or the answers may raise new questions. It may result in a decision that the research should go ahead; identify that the research question is wrong and that further research or even a new start is needed; or that the project is not viable at all.

Following this process should identify the focus of the research but, once a decision has been taken to continue, the project design will reflect the specifics of stages in the research cycle. It should also contain several other elements: a structure including governance arrangements through which accountable decisions and actions can be overseen; a plan for carrying out the different research activities through to dissemination and evaluation; and involvement and communications strategies. Patients and the public should be involved in planning and also playing different roles in research activities; these may be different patients and members of the public at different times. Whether individuals are involved in governance, dissemination and evaluation will depend on what appropriate skills, and confidence, they can bring into play. Here, the involvement strategy and its communication will be vital to ensure clarity and build trust.

Another important element of the project specification is the scope, what should be included and what should be left out. Decisions may be based on manageability, achievability or research programme or funding criteria.

Case Example 2   Setting the Scope

A statutory organisation that is the local consumer champion for all health and social care provision was planning a research project on local GP services. In England there had been increasing concerns about the GP service including access to appointments with GPs and to their surgeries, and what happened when patients were referred to hospitals or therapists for treatment. The original proposal was to cover all the issues raised in a single project, but a patient who was also an experienced project manager advised them that if the research was to be done on anything other than a superficial level, the volume of work would be too great, it would take a long time, and the findings might not be sufficiently robust for the providers to take action. The project was divided into two stages to run consecutively: the first looking at the interaction of GP surgeries with patients, and the second at the interaction between GP surgeries and the professionals and organisations to whom they referred patients. Information gathered from patients and the GP practices during the first stage informed the second. The findings have been widely circulated among the service providers.

Enforcing the scope also provides an opportunity for ideas which are interesting but do not fit within the current project to be set aside for discussion and evaluation as potential new projects at a later date.

3.4   How to Be Involved

This brings us to a discussion of the wider involvement roles of patients and the public throughout the life of the project. In Chap. 1 we referred to several examples of involvement roles and activities suggested by the UK's NHS. Figure 3.2 illustrates the organisational hierarchy of involvement roles and activities.

ROLE ONE:
A small group of PPI expert advisors in the key project steering group.

ROLE TWO
A PPI advisory group, maybe mostly of patients and the public, to advise regularly on aspects of the project

ROLE THREE
People taking part in deliberative PPI workshops to inform the research. They might also be recruited for the two roles above.

ROLE FOUR
Any people who might offer a range of experiences and views to directly inform the deliberations of the groups above.

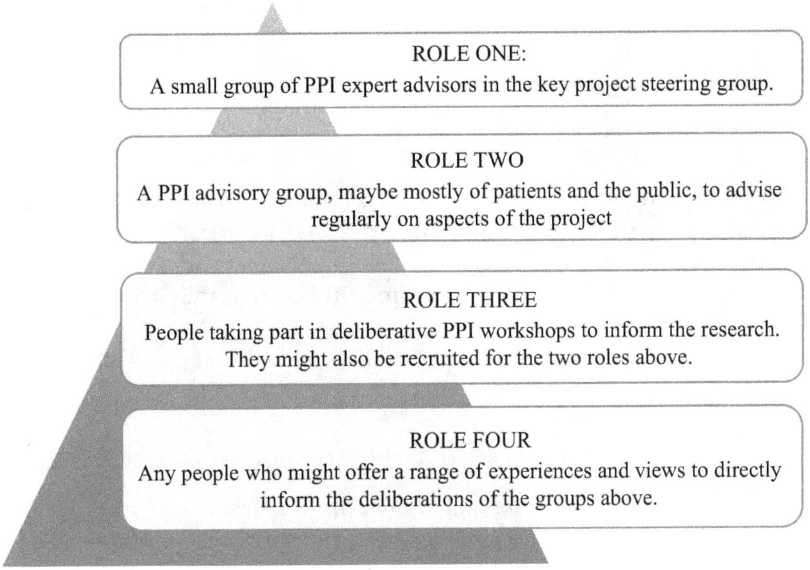

Fig. 3.2   Roles and activities for PPI involvement in research

At the most basic level, people can contribute their experiences and views by responding to surveys to provide information, and consultations to provide opinions about what research topics are relevant. They can attend one-off deliberative workshops or regular working or reference groups to define research topics, interventions or research plans, or as part of research activities. They can sit on an advisory panel of experts by experience, or become expert advisors who work alongside various other types of expert (see NHS England 2017: 8). The last two roles are commonly used to involve lay people across the NHS. Figure 3.2 indicates the increasing levels of expertise and responsibility involvement may require. Any or all of these roles may be suitable for a particular research project depending on the design both of decision-making in general, and patient and public involvement in particular. However, if any of the four types of role described above were to be used as the only form of involvement in a project, this would be unlikely to reliably cover all the types of PPI input a project is likely to need to guarantee that its findings will be sufficiently relevant or robust. When used in combination from decision-making to evaluation, these and other forms of involvement can enable project teams to design involvement in a way that ensures that the skills and breadth of views needed are available at every stage. However, the practicalities these roles bring with them need to be thought through so that they work within each project. The section which follows will help in thinking through the basics for making them work for you.

Key questions 3.1
What questions do you need to ask when making contact with potential lay members of the research team to ensure that you have the right skills mix?
How would you decide who to bring on board at the beginning of the project?
How would you decide who to allocate to which role?

3.5   The Practicalities of Involvement

In the rest of this chapter, we will discuss the practicalities of involvement. These can be complicated to identify and the solutions for resolving any dilemmas they raise will depend on the type of people being involved and the nature of the research. For example, the requirements for service design with a lot of user involvement are very different from those with a large technical element. We will start with those practicalities, access and the use of language, that apply throughout all involvement and then go on to look at collaboration, communication and evaluation, ending by spelling out the issues surrounding the cost of involvement. We will refer throughout to the hierarchy of involvement described in Fig. 3.2 to unpick and illustrate some of the layers of complexity.

Collaboration can only happen when the needs, wishes and expectations of the range of PPI members being involved in the research team are taken into account. There is no ready short cut to finding out what these are; the researchers leading the project need to directly discuss them with the PPI members. The researchers may have an idea of the general requirements of a project and the principles of PPI, but it can be dangerous to make assumptions about needs based on what is known about the background of the members. Making such assumptions can lead to underestimating what needs to be put in place for people to enable them to participate physically or intellectually, or indeed to underestimate the high level of contribution lay people can make to the research because of rather than despite their different experience of additional needs. Getting the practicalities wrong can undermine any relationship of trust and confidence before the work has even started. It is unlikely that you will get everything right the whole time. The devil is in the detail.

Case Example 3   Working with Disabled People
A statutory organisation that is the consumer champion for all health and social care provision in its area wished to review the provision of housing for people with learning disabilities or autism. At first it considered involving volunteers who worked with it regularly, but it decided that this was unlikely to gain the information it needed. Instead it decided to work with trustees and members of a voluntary organisation that supported disabled people. The new volunteers defined the questions that they would need to ask the people living and working in the housing and these were agreed by both organisations. The training on what would happen when the volunteers visited the housing was facilitated by a member of staff who they already knew. After the visits, the experienced volunteers would normally be asked to write up a report themselves, but in this case facilitators met the volunteers soon after they had left the housing, discussed what they had found and wrote up the information gathered for them before agreeing the final version.

Two over-arching factors may shape people's ability to take part: physical access, and the use of language. Both need to be considered from the very beginning. Failing to get them right can result in some people being excluded.

It is likely that at some stage you will need the patients and members of the public you are involving to attend meetings. There is no shortage of good practice around the basic requirements: level access for wheelchairs, but also space to move around easily, toilets for the disabled and hearing loops. Most organisations have a set of guidelines. But it is not just about the accessibility of the building itself; people need to be able to travel there. Not everyone can drive or has access to a car, nor can they necessarily afford a taxi, so being on a public transport route helps. There are also practical, softer, factors that give contributors access within the wider environment of the project. If people invited have school-age children, they may wish to meet during school hours and allow time to drop their children off and collect them later. A carer's activities may be limited by the opening hours of a day centre or the number of hours, and cost, of making alternative care arrangements. A public sector organisation arranged an event to explore the needs of carers, intending to redesign a number of services to better meet their needs, but few carers were able to attend because it used a hotel in the country several miles outside the city where they were based. Attendance was further limited by the fact that the event was planned to last a whole day.

Groups of people with experience of living with a given condition may have very specific requirements if they are to be involved effectively. The best source of advice here is the people who helped you to find those you are involving. They will know the additional requirements regarding accessible accommodation and additional facilities, but also what types of support they need. The following are just some of the questions you need to ask:

- Is there somewhere they already meet that would be suitable?
- What additional facilities do they need?
- Will they need to be accompanied by carers or support workers?
- Do you need to work with specialist facilitators who understand their needs, and would working with someone with whom they are already familiar be helpful?
- Are there additional communications needs? These will be covered in more detail in a later section.

- Do the timing and duration of the meeting need to be taken into account?
- Will you need a greater number of breaks than usual?
- Will they need specialist transport arrangements?
- And if you are using community transport, is there enough available to carry the number of people you want to invite?

A review to find out what factors might help or hinder involving older residents in research into care homes highlighted that all of these were often relevant in this case. (Backhouse et al. 2016)

Such arrangements will inevitably incur additional costs you need to factor into your research budget. Handling such costs is covered at the end of this section,

The use of language is an important, but often ignored, aspect of accessibility. Plain English can help not only patients and the public but professionals coming from different backgrounds as well. As we explained in Chap. 1, different people use the same term to mean different things, and different terms to mean the same thing. A lay person who has not hesitated to ask for explanations of acronyms and technical terms has often found that professionals have approached them afterwards to thank them because they did not know what was meant either. Plain English not only avoids confusion but also is a matter of simple courtesy. Any project will involve a range of vocabulary that is specific to it and even an expert advisor will not necessarily be familiar with all of it. Producing a glossary helps.

However, the needs around language go further than plain English. When working in a deprived area where education standards are poor, it may help to take the average local reading age into consideration. People with learning difficulties may need documents in easy-read versions and they may need support workers present if they attend meetings. A public sector organisation carrying out research on plans to change the way in which health services were delivered wanted to find out the priorities of the local population. They produced standard and easy-read versions of their consultation document. In the latter, they had used cartoons to explain examples of how services might work in the future. They decided that this approach was so much clearer that they used it in both versions.

People from ethnic minorities may need interpreters who speak their own language. This need should be explored very early in the project. Even those who speak good English may not be familiar with the technical language that will be used during the research. Deaf people regard signing as a language in its own right and also work with interpreters. Both will need interpreters when attending meetings as individuals or in groups. When doing research on difficulties deaf people have in accessing services, a statutory organisation that is the consumer champion for all health and social care provision in their area met them in their club with staff from the local voluntary organisation that supports them as joint facilitators and deaf interpreters from a specialist service. The deaf people produced a video to help disseminate the findings.

It is important to remember that access of this type applies to roles at all levels in research projects. For accessibility topics to consider for involvement, see Table 3.2.

Table 3.2   Accessibility topics to consider for involvement

Role one	Key to consider: training needed for the chair and all group members. Are people involved in expert roles sufficiently prepared and trained to take part comfortably in the discussions; and are meeting roles clear to all those attending so that the expert advisors are less likely to feel patronised or excluded?
Role two	Key to consider: individual needs. Can people take part at the times allocated, and do they require transport or child care support? Is the length of the meeting and number of breaks appropriate? Are the documents appropriate for the PPI members?
Role three	Key to consider: physical access needs such as wheelchair access, ways to get to the venue, linguistic barriers if English is not the first language of those involved and cultural obstacles such as unsuitable days or dates
Role four	Key to consider: how to promote the survey or consultation so as to engage the people you want to respond; the appropriate media, for example, electronic, paper or interviews; and how much time to give to respond

Moving on from accessibility, we must to look at the arrangements that need to be put in place to achieve collaborative working. The preparatory phase of the research will have identified the structure and governance arrangements for the project, how the work will be done and who will be involved at each stage. The structure may include some form of steering or management group which should include PPI representatives; a PPI advisory or reference group; possibly a group of expert advisors; deliberative groups, working or task and finish groups to cover specific aspects of the project; and arrangements for disseminating the findings and evaluation. These reflect the potential involvement roles set out in Sect. 3.4 and PPI members should be involved at all levels. The precise structure will depend on the nature of the research.

Effective involvement is dependent on the ability of researchers to make connections and work collaboratively with patients and the public, the PPI members of the research team. To achieve this it is important to ensure clarity concerning the roles, responsibilities and scope for action of each group being involved in the project structure and how they interact with each other. The governance will need to describe the formal decision-making structure: which groups and individuals take decisions and how these and other information are communicated. All this should be clearly understood by everybody involved.

When considering PPI, it will be necessary to decide how many of what types of person are needed, in which part of the structure, and what knowledge and expertise they will need to work at each level. Support and training should be provided which is suited to the background of the people involved. They will need to be talked through their own individual role, how it fits into the structure of the project and how the information they provide will be used. They will also need to know what will be expected of them, and be introduced to the people with whom they will be working. However, this needs to be a two-way, collaborative conversation: members of the research team need to understand what the PPI representatives expect, what they hope to see from the project and what they, personally, would like to get out of it. People need to reach consensus on this and to document it.

Communications and building relationships are essential to the success of research. At the point when the research is getting under way, the members of the project team with responsibilities for these areas should identify any specific support needs PPI members may have, including any questions relating to access and personal needs, together with any additional training they may require have to help them fulfil their roles in this project. This should be done with tact and respect. It may be helpful to repeat this process and check support needs at intervals during the course of the project as people's circumstances can change. People taking part in a deliberative workshop or a particular working group may need a specialist form of facilitation. Members of a PPI advisory group will need an explanation of how their particular committee works, where it fits into the project, or some of the technical details that the participant will come across.

Particular care should be taken with regard to committees, which can be daunting to even the most experienced participants. Accessibility, timing, the use of language and the possible need for an interpreter are all important, but the sheer volume of paper produced can also cause problems. Participants without the right technical knowledge and experience may not be used to this and may need additional time to prepare; this is not always easy if the project is working to tight deadlines. It is also helpful to check if a participant has access to appropriate IT and a suitable printer. Some NHS boards offer lay representatives a briefing session to prepare them before the beginning of each session.

Key questions 3.2
Your research project is likely to generate a large volume of written materials. How can you ensure that these will be meaningful and manageable for your lay members?

Surveys and consultations may be used throughout a research project, not just in the preparatory stage, as a means of gathering information and opinions. All the advice relating to accessibility of location, timing and language applies here. Both surveys and consultations need to be focused; you need to be clear about what information you need, and decide how large a sample size you need for your findings to be robust. As a basic principle, the longer the survey, the less likely people are to complete it. You may need to involve patients and the public to check the survey and its presentation before you use it to make sure it is appropriate to the audience. And you need to think about how you are going to analyse the responses.

The next question is where to find the people who are going to supply the information you are seeking. If you are working with a service provider, such as a hospital or an organisation that provides care in the community, it may be able to help. However, caution needs to be exercised with some voluntary organisations. There is a concern that those who see only the people with the greatest need may provide their own views of what they think is needed on that basis rather than giving you access to a wide range of people with lived experience.

Collaboration is also about culture and building relationships, a people-based approach. It is good practice to bring everybody, both researchers and patients and the public, together at the beginning of a project to build understanding by introducing everybody to the nature of the project, how it will work and who the key people are. But communications should be maintained throughout the course of the research to keep everyone informed about progress; for the researchers to be sure that the way they are working with PPI participants is giving them the information they need; and to give the participants the chance to talk about how they feel the work is progressing. It is always possible to change ways of working to produce a better result.

> *Exercise 3.2*
> Consider this question: What communications processes might you need to establish to ensure that you can keep in touch with the lay members of your project?

For many, what they wish to experience through their involvement in PPI reaches beyond their role in the research structure. They want to feel a genuine part of the project, to know how their information has been used, whether their advice has been listened to, how it fits into the final product and what the findings are. This means that communications should include feedback loops rather than going straight up and down through the hierarchy of the project. If, for example, researchers are unclear about the significance of comments, then it may be helpful if they go back to the PPI members for further discussions to achieve a shared view. Failure to communicate how information has been used and whether advice has been listened to can be a source of great frustration and disappointment. A carer involved in a project on the discharge of hospital patients was concerned about the effect the new approach could have on their fellow carers, but after their initial contribution the work was taken back by the professionals and they had no idea whether or not they had been listened to or whether the changes were being evaluated to see what effect they were having on carers.

For collaborative practice based on shared understandings of decision-making processes, roles, information and consequences, see Table 3.3 and for communication practices to support involvement, see Table 3.4.

Table 3.3 Collaborative practice based on shared understandings of decision-making processes, roles, information and consequences

Role one	Everyone should understand clearly how decisions are taken, who has the responsibility to implement them and what the consequences will be if they are not implemented
Role two	Everyone should understand clearly the nature and function of the group, what people can expect and what is expected from them
Role three	A people-focused approach should be used to keep the way a group works open to changes proposed by those involved while keeping a focus on the topic
Role four	Carefully designed, analysed and interpreted surveys can inform collaborative work

Table 3.4 Communication practices to support involvement

Role one	Key to consider: how information is processed. Awards committees dealing with thousands of pages of applications may need to consider their practices when involving patients or members of the public who are not used to dealing with large volumes of information
Role two	Key to consider: how information is presented, recorded, shared and stored. Minutes, updates and invitations should be timely
Role three	Key to consider: the way people are invited, the information they receive to prepare them, and the way the meeting is followed up
Role four	Key to consider: the language and format of any survey critically influences how well people can and will be involved

Communication, which will be part of the structure of every project, is central to involving people as it is the means through which people deal with each other, exchange information and so build shared understandings. The practical details to consider here are the explicit ways in which any group collaborating for research is communicating: What are people saying to each other and to the wider world, in writing and in conversation? What language are they using, is it respectful and can it be comfortably used by everyone? Is it fit for purpose? Does it define and help people share information in a transparent manner on the topics to which they need access if they are to be able to take part in discussions and decision-making? This means that you may need to check how documents are prepared, circulated and stored. Does everyone have the access that they need, including sufficient time to enable them to understand key documents well enough to consider the topics they cover? Similarly, when working in groups, are topics introduced and discussions facilitated in ways which enable everyone to take part, including those with speech or sensory disabilities? Less visible may be preparing and debriefing PPI members to encourage them to see their contributions to communicating as having equal value; to support them to make these contributions; and to reflect on how important they are and how they may be affected by the current arrangements for communication. A health organisation involved in introducing large-scale changes to how services were to be delivered in the community arranged a meeting of patient representatives and voluntary organisations to discuss what was planned. The area covered was very mixed with relatively affluent areas alongside others that were economically disadvantaged. Representatives of patient participation groups from the deprived areas complained that some of the documents were too long and their content was too complex for them to be able to comment. This highlights the importance of the various opportunities and arrangements for being involved in evaluating the processes and products of research, including involvement itself, which we now go on to consider in more detail. For topics to consider regarding evaluation processes, see Table 3.5.

Table 3.5 Practices in being involved in evaluating processes and products of research

Role one	Key to consider: whether the steering group should oversee project evaluation and commission independent evaluation including reviewing the effectiveness of the steering group
Role two	Key to consider: advisory groups may work well to review research findings and consider what difference they may make to knowledge and actions
Role three	Key to consider: deliberative workshops can be used to consider specific evaluation questions
Role four	Key to consider: while there is not usually a direct role for people who have responded to surveys in evaluating the project, it is nonetheless feasible

If we want to know how, when and to what extent PPI has been part of a particular research project, it is not enough for research teams or even PPI members to assert in general terms that patients and the public 'have been involved'. Evaluation of such involvement needs to be comprehensive. The project's steering group, which, ideally, should include PPI members, should commission, oversee and review any such evaluation which must be tailored to the people and circumstances of the particular research project. This may be done internally or commissioned from an external provider depending on the scope and complexity of the research. Processes need to be put in place for a group of PPI and other research team members to evaluate, or contribute to the evaluation of the processes, products and experiences of their involvement. In Table 3.5 we summarise the range of practicalities to consider here. The evaluation should review the research findings and, in particular, consider what differences their application might make to knowledge, practice and actions in the wider community. To achieve this will mean finding ways to enable people to decide how to identify the differences made and consider the strength of their effect. One way to do this could be to set up working groups of PPI members to review the effects of findings set by set. In addition a wider group of PPI members could be encouraged to complete surveys giving their own views.

The evaluation could be extended to reviewing the effectiveness and experiences of PPI in the research in addition to the findings. The extent to which this can be achieved will depend on: whether a two-way, collaborative discussion took place in the early stages of the project; whether members of the research team and PPI participants reached consensus on the team's descriptions of the PPI participants' roles and the expectations of both groups of how these would work; and how this consensus was recorded. If these arrangements are in place, an evaluation of what happened in practice will go some way to 'complete the feedback loop' (Mathie et al. 2018) recently highlighted in the UK as making an important contribution to PPI becoming more integrated in and having greater impact on the world of research.

A way of reviewing the evaluation processes themselves is also needed. One way to do this may be to hold deliberative workshops which include PPI members and other stakeholders able to develop and refine further evaluation questions and the answers to them.

The final practicality we will discuss is the question of making payments for involvement. All the other practicalities we have identified take up people's time and may incur costs for transport and care support as they are being taken outside the context of their everyday lives. It is vital to recognise and address this, not least because many people who are living with long-term conditions relevant to health research or are caring for people who live with them often have very limited financial resources or access to benefits. They should not be left out of pocket or put their livelihoods at risk by being involved. Payment to PPI participants is a practicality that needs to be considered on a case by case basis; it is important to remember that PPI participants involved at very different levels may have similar types of needs. What they are should be identified in the initial conversations. For the practicalities of payments for involvement, see Table 3.6.

Table 3.6 Practicalities of payments for involvement

Role one	According to NHS guidance, expert members may receive involvement payments to acknowledge the value of their input Caution But accepting such payments for people receiving welfare benefits (e.g. in the UK) may result in loss of benefit or change personal tax liability
Role two	NHS England currently suggests reimbursing expenses but not paying for involvement. It is unclear if expenses for care for dependents, for example, children, could be reimbursed without resulting in changes in benefits awarded or in tax liability
Role three	There is usually no payment for time and expertise, however, incentives such as giving a lottery ticket for taking part, which may win a prize, have been considered
Role four	There is usually no payment for this, albeit incentives such as the possibility of winning a prize for taking part have been considered

Making payments for involvement provides a striking example of why practicalities have to be worked out in detail at an early stage so that they work for each research project, the people involved and their circumstances. It may seem to be common sense that PPI members should not be left out of pocket in any way, that it is respectful to clearly value their effort and expertise, but there are many things to consider when deciding whether and how such payments should be made.

In many ways reimbursing expenses seems the most obvious cost to be reimbursed as being involved should not lead to people incurring financial costs to themselves. There is widespread agreement that paying such travel and subsistence costs to, from and during involvement activities should be routine. However, there are other considerations to bear in mind here.

It is not always clear if there are ways of paying for the costs of care for dependents such as children or disabled family members without this resulting in changes in benefits awarded or in tax liability. Expert PPI participants may be awarded involvement payments to formally acknowledge the value of their input. However, where people are already receiving welfare or other means-tested benefits, as may happen within the UK, receiving such payments may result in people losing their existing benefits or changes to their personal tax liability. In both these cases, there may be regulations or even legislation which require people to self-report any such changes to the benefits agency or to the national tax authorities. There may be similar regulations which require organisations involving PPI members in research to report taxable payments or gifts in kind. NHS England therefore currently suggests not paying for involvement, other than in role one, although local authorities do make such payments.

There is usually no payment for time and expertise; however, incentives such as giving a lottery ticket for taking part, which may win a prize, have been considered. In some countries, such as the US, cash payments up to $500 can be made for taking part in research without reporting these. However, in other countries such as Denmark, no payments can be made in connection with taking part in research, which must be seen to have no connection with financial interests.

3.6   What Can Go Wrong and How We Can Prepare to Deal with It

We all plan for things to go well. Research processes are carefully designed and, as we have seen, are open to external scrutiny to ensure that nothing goes wrong, for instance in relation to ethics, financial management, governance and training. However, we would be neglecting our responsibilities if we worked and planned only on the assumption that nothing ever goes wrong. So every project needs to put appropriate plans in place to deal with this when it happens.

One set of issues can arise if someone involved in a project, as a patient or member of the public, is harmed or distressed as a result of activities or people they encounter while being involved. This may include being abused or bullied by someone in a powerful position either within the project or in groups or places that participants encounter in the process of involvement. People may also be distressed or be put in difficult positions if they raise ethical concerns that are not followed up, or if they witness poor practice.

Issues may also arise if a person involved in a project as a patient or a member of the public behaves inappropriately, uses abusive language, offers false or misleading information, makes threats that unreasonably undermine the project, does not respect confidentiality or does something else which can affect the reputation of others involved.

There are some established practices that can protect from harm and support patients participating in research which is being reviewed by ethics panels, such as making sure that ways a participant can complain or express concerns are clearly identified and communicated to everyone involved in the project at an early stage. If lay people are employed as peer researchers, working within an organisation, what they do will be regulated by employment law and they will also be able to call on any form of protection that is operated by the organisation. However, such arrangements are not currently routinely put in place in every type of research activity. Nor would they necessarily be appropriate in patient and public involvement in research when participants are not formally employed and are acting as volunteers. So a tailored approach will need to be thought through and discussed with everyone likely to be affected.

We argue that in planning for any event when things go wrong, two elements are essential and should be made part of any organisational policy. First of all, there has to be a clear and transparent way for anyone involved in the project to raise concerns with one or more people designated to take responsibility for dealing appropriately with those concerns. The people designated to take responsibility should, in the first instance, be those managing the project. If it is not appropriate for them to address the concern because of its nature, or they cannot resolve the issue, their place should be taken by a senior manager in the research organisation or the organisation hosting the research. If the concern still cannot be resolved, then the funding body or an equivalent body resourcing the research should take over responsibility. Identifying and providing details of the appropriate contacts should be addressed when setting up the project. This information should be given to anyone taking on roles connected with public or patient involvement in research as part of their introduction to the project. There may be some cases where PPI members do not feel able to raise a concern or wish to see it treated as a formal complaint. Or they may have experienced distress in other ways. There should therefore also be signposting to contacts who can provide suitable support. To enable this to happen, as with planning for ethics (see Chap. 4), the whole research team including PPI members may need to anticipate the kinds of distress that being involved in the research could raise.

Secondly, it is usual practice in volunteer management to have role descriptions and agreements in place that explain the responsibilities of the volunteers. These often include sections on how any perceived misconduct of volunteers can and should be dealt with including suspending and terminating involvement. They also usually include participants' responsibilities to treat confidentially personal and other information gained in the course of being involved. Public and personal liability should also be clarified.

In summary, it is essential that we consider what safeguards should be and have been put in place to protect those involved as patients and members of the public in research. These should be communicated in such a way that PPI members can see any such arrangements as transparent and that accountability for deciding on them is clear, so that they have confidence in playing their part as fully involved partners.

3.7   Summary and Conclusions

In line with our approach to equipping PPI members to build their independent contribution to involvement, this chapter has been designed to 'prompt thinking' and to help develop processes for planning involvement that engage everyone. A fuller checklist of the issues and practicalities is given in Chap. 6. This chapter has aimed to illustrate how patient and public involvement in research practice flows from clear principles to understand and then to anticipate who, when and how to involve participants in differing research projects and partnerships. We see sound patient and public involvement as needing to promote inclusion. Therefore, we have taken as our starting point 'who' being everyone and, ideally, people with direct experience. 'When' must ideally begin with the first thoughts about research. 'How' is to treat everyone with the appropriate care and respect. In turn, this means openly acknowledging that things can go wrong and therefore equipping people to know how to deal with this, too.

REFERENCES

Backhouse, T., Kenkmann, A., Lane, K., Penhale, B., Poland, F., & Killett, A. (2016). Older care-home residents as collaborators or advisors in research: A systematic review. *Age and Ageing*. https://doi.org/10.1093/ageing/afv201.

Jacobs, L., Komashie, A., Lombardo, C., & Clarke, G. (2017). *Patient and public involvement (PPI) in research handbook*. Cambridge: CLAHRC EoE.

Keenan, J., Poland, F., Boote, J., Howe, A., Wythe, H., Varley, A., Vicary, P., Irvine, L., & Wellings, A. (2019). 'We're passengers sailing in the same ship, but we have our own berths to sleep in': Evaluating patient and public involvement within a regional research programme: An action research project informed by normalisation process theory. *PLoS One, 14*(5), e0215953.

Mathie, E., Wythe, H., Munday, D., Millac, P., Rhodes, G., Roberts, N., et al. (2018). Reciprocal relationships and the importance of feedback in patient and public involvement: A mixed methods study. *Health Expectations, 21*(5), 899–908.

NHS England. (2017). *Working with our patient and public voice (PPV) partners – Reimbursing expenses and paying involvement payments (v2)*. Redditch: NHS England.

NIHR. (2018). *National standards for public involvement in research V1 March 2018*. NIHR.

NIHR INVOLVE. (2012). *Briefing notes for researchers: Public involvement in NHS, public health and social care research*. Eastleigh: INVOLVE.

Nuffield Department of Primary Care Health Sciences. (2015). *Guide for researchers working with patient and public involvement (PPI) representatives*. Oxford: Nuffield Department of Primary Care Health Sciences.

Poland, F., Charlesworth, G., Leung, P., & Birt, L. (2019). Embedding patient and public involvement: Managing tacit and explicit expectations. *Health Expectations, 22*(6), 1231–1239.

Turk, A., Boylan, A. M., & Locock, L. (approx 2017). *A researcher's guide to patient and public involvement*. Oxford: Oxford NIHR Biomedical Research Centre.

CHAPTER 4

PPI in Research Ethics and Ethics in PPI

We set out in earlier chapters key reasons why we need good PPI and what we can do to organise this. However, we also need to understand the importance of ethics in regulating the effects of research design and practice on the safety and wellbeing of people, and the importance of PPI in ensuring that community viewpoints and voices inform the full recognition of these effects. *"Since it was founded 60 years ago, ethics has been at the heart of WHO's [World Health Organisation] mission to protect and promote the global community's health"* (Coleman et al. 2008: 578).

Attending to ethics helps us identify the moral principles we need to follow in choosing and planning our actions. The laws that regulate research practice include universal guidelines that enforce the ethical conduct applicable to all research activities and everyone affected by research. As these include PPI contributions, the guidelines must also be applied to patients and the public. However, importantly, these PPI activities will also help ensure that the way in which ethical principles are applied in research design and decision-making makes it relevant to people who are research participants or who will be affected by its findings.

In this chapter we will travel through the landscape of ethics in research to define the role of PPI within the journey from research ideas to practice. We will explore how specific laws, guidelines and organisations have been developed to help us understand ways in which ethics is brought into research practice and regulated. Since the 1940s, a number of countries have set up organisations in law to regulate ethics: for example, the Health

Research Authority in the UK; the National Commission for the Protection of Human Subjects of Biomedical and Behavioral Research in the USA; and the Uganda National Council for Science and Technology (UNCST) in Uganda. We will then look at how we ourselves can decide what ethical principles and procedures we may need to apply in practice when working on a research project.

We will start by finding out what ethics is and why it matters in health and social care. We go on to look at how local ethics panels approve the ethical arrangements in research designs for projects, how we can deal with ethical issues that arise in practice, and ways to build ethics into your designs to gain the approval of the ethics panel that will consider your planning. This could include, for example, designing a consent form in such a way that it ensures that the people likely to take part in your project will have access to the information they need to give their full, voluntary consent. We will consider how PPI can be part of deciding what may constitute ethical planning and action in different research situations. Finally, we will explore the dimension of power in shaping assumptions about what is good, relevant or harmful and how this can affect what people and topics may be included when considering ethics in research, and how PPI may help in recognising and balancing their consequences.

By the end of this chapter, you should know what the key ethical requirements may be, where to seek relevant guidance and how to apply it to PPI, and how PPI can help strengthen ethical practice in research. We again remind you to be cautious about any guidance that suggests that there is an automatic and widespread consensus about what ethical issues doing PPI raises and how these may best be managed. This chapter will therefore look at:

- Connecting ethics, everyday actions and research activities
- Why do laws exist to govern ethics in research?
- What is lay involvement in research governance?
- What is lay involvement in research ethics?
- What are the ethics of lay involvement?
- How may people and issues be included and excluded?
- Ethics and power
- Identifying and deciding ethical issues in practice

4.1   Connecting Ethics, Everyday Actions and Research Activities

The foremost principle of medical or scientific practice, including research practice, is the well-known saying from the Hippocratic oath: 'First do no harm'. However, to understand why this may be important, what we think is harmful and who may be doing harm, particularly in relation to PPI, is not as simple as these few words suggest. There are three commonly used ways of thinking about how ethics helps us judge whether our actions are good and worthwhile: 'consequentialist', 'duty-related' and 'virtue-related' (Kaptein and Wempe 2002). One way to think about needing to be aware of ethics in PPI is to recognise that our own and researchers' actions will always have consequences, which can affect us and other people, who include the wider community; this is a consequentialist approach. We judge the effects of what happens in terms of how far they may be morally acceptable, including whether they lead to harms or benefits. What happens when we do not judge this carefully was illustrated painfully by a study of disabled peoples' lives in a care home (Miller and Gwynne 1972). This study was later critiqued by the disability activist Paul Hunt, who referred to researchers as 'parasite people' (Hunt 1981).

Because people are different, live diverse lives and have access to differing resources, what may be harmful to some people may benefit others. As PPI members can bring diverse views about what moral beliefs about harms and benefits may be relevant in particular cases for any given research project, they can ensure the research can look beyond researchers' assumptions about what may be right and relevant.

Case Example 4a   Pregnant Women and Smoking
A researcher studying ways to encourage pregnant women to stop smoking has read the literature but has never smoked themselves, nor been pregnant. PPI members who have smoked and been pregnant will have a range of potentially diverse ideas on what interventions may have acceptable, or distressing consequences.

Another way to think about reasons for bringing ethics into PPI is to relate them to the duties we all share to take the right actions and avoid wrong actions regardless of their consequences. This approach takes into account the moral responsibilities that apply to us all and will therefore apply to both research and PPI. This may help when we want to clearly set out and take into account what we know is important for treating people and communities equitably, fairly and respectfully.

Again, because people are diverse they may also have different views about what the universal ethical principles are that always need to be applied to practice. You will therefore also need to work at finding out what other principles and practices people think should be applied in a specific case to identify the ethics of the research.

Case Example 4b   Pregnant Women and Smoking, the PPI Member View
The researcher seen above knows from the literature about ways to encourage pregnant women to stop smoking drawing on different knowledge from PPI members who have smoked and been pregnant. The PPI members may bring diverse ideas on how to clearly describe interventions to make people aware of their potential side effects to ensure they are fully informed before they decide on taking part in research to test them.

A third way of thinking about ethics concerns how people interact with each other; it is about recognising ethical behaviour as something people do because they are people of good character or 'virtue'. This thinking allows us to include many ways of defining what is good in people and respectfully recognising that there are many cultural beliefs, practices and experiences that can shape a person's desire to take responsibility for acting well and therefore to decide to act well, including in planning and undertaking research. This is relevant to how researchers and PPI members may work with each other to approach ethical issues and therefore need to find ways of listening to each other to take account of differences that may relate to gender, ethnicity or socio-economic circumstances.

Case Example 4c Pregnant Women and Smoking, Cultural Influences
The case seen above of the researcher who draws knowledge from the literature about ways to encourage pregnant women to stop smoking and the PPI members who have themselves smoked and been pregnant, highlights that the PPI members may have very different ideas about whether they see women who smoke during pregnancy, including themselves, as good or worthwhile people.

Each of these ways of thinking about acting ethically shows that we will need to find a way to judge how we recognise research as producing good and desirable experiences and outcomes for individuals and the wider community. Because people are not the same as each other, involving lay people in considering what ethics are relevant in research is essential to ensure processes of ethical regulation take different views and standpoints into account. Furthermore, if PPI volunteers play a part in shaping research, then ethical principles will also apply to what they do and how they are treated in research activities in which they are involved. What we have set out here is a way to identify what ethical approaches PPI members may be taking themselves, and how others they are involved with may be considering what ethical issues are relevant.

4.2 Why do Laws Exist to Govern Ethics in Research

Over the last hundred years, strict legal enforcement of clear and universal standards of ethics in research has come to be seen as essential in giving permission for any research to take place which involves people and gains access to information about them. This came about because the twentieth century revealed many terrible and tragic examples of what health researchers felt able to do in the absence of laws on ethics or regulation. Some health researchers not only neglected to protect patients but also, in some cases, deliberately harmed them for the purposes of research to observe the consequences. We saw notorious examples that took place over several years and affected thousands of people. In response to the deliberately harmful and coercive research undertaken extensively in Nazi Germany, the 'Nuremberg Code' of research ethics was drawn up in 1948. Later the 'Helsinki Declaration' explicitly required that all people taking part in research should only do so if they had given their fully informed consent. This meant being able to ascertain that participants had been enabled to take part of their own free will and without being coerced in any way, that is they were participating voluntarily. It also meant that all procedures planned and carried out in any research study had to be independently reviewed to ensure that they were ethical.

Yet it was not only dictatorships that sanctioned appalling research actions, even in quite recent times. Between 1932 and 1972, the US Public Health Service conducted the Tuskegee Syphilis Study in which hundreds of Afro-American men were deliberately infected with syphilis.

Having had to agree that it was not controversial to have to regulate against such harmful practices, most countries now have substantial legislation to do this. Most importantly, these changes now make it the individual responsibility of every researcher to be seen to exercise due concern for research ethics when they are involved in carrying out research. This means that they must first and foremost protect patients and the public and must never give higher priority to their research interests. This does not just entail not causing people physical or mental harm but also not wasting their time or not leaving them with the impression of having had their time wasted because they were offered research which was badly designed or irrelevant. The principle underpinning this responsibility is neither an optional extra nor an arbitrary bureaucratic hurdle. It has emerged from intrinsic experiences and hard-won lessons, and it is a critical principle in recognising that research is sound.

To ensure that the ethics of a research project can be independently reviewed, the legislation to regulate health research requires independent ethics committees to be set up which bring health professionals together with people who are not members of health professions. This explicitly encourages including lay viewpoints. These committees are responsible for protecting the rights to wellbeing of people involved in health research and of wider communities that may be affected by research outcomes. They are also responsible for assuring the public that the people involved in making these judgements are qualified to do so, and that the people involved in running the research have appropriate expertise, resources and means of informing and gaining consent from people considering taking part.

In the UK, these committees are called Research Ethics Committees (RECs), and are part of the NHS. In Finland, there are relatively few RECs but these are part of the legal system itself. In the US, there are many RECs, which run in private as well as public hospitals; sometimes there are several in one hospital. Guidelines in some countries are more advisory. 'In some cases, there are specific provisions relating to particular indigenous populations. In New Zealand, the importance of ensuring that research related to healthcare contributes to health development in Maori communities has been recognised' (Maori Health Committee of the Health Research Council of New Zealand 2010). Similarly, in Australia the National Health and Medical Research Council (NHMRC) has addressed the ethical issues that arise for research related to health in Aboriginal and Torres Strait Islanders (National Health and Medical Research Council of Australia, updated 2018).

Earlier in this chapter, we have seen that the key ways of thinking about ethics provide us with sound reasons for understanding how PPI can provide extra oversight and improve ethical practice as well as making the research process and products more widely relevant and accessible.

However, as described in Chap. 1, there is a moral or democratic argument for involving those affected by research in processes which govern the ethics of that research and guard against ethical risks for PPI volunteers who become involved in conducting ethical reviews as currently organised (see also Coleman et al. 2009). We will explore these in more detail when looking at lay involvement in research governance in general and research ethics in particular.

Exercise 4.1
In a research project to examine work with people with learning disabilities to enable them to self-manage their healthy eating, what ethical issues might need to be managed in the research design?

4.3   What Is Lay Involvement in Research Governance?

Lay members can now be involved in a variety of roles in organisations or activities which oversee research. These include ensuring research is responsibly regulated, has robust governance, and is subjected to morally regulated, ethical review. In the UK, the Care Act, 2014, has given the Health Research Authority (HRA)-specific legal responsibility for regulating public involvement in the area of research governance and for providing guidance on their involvement.

> *We could not operate without our network of around 1,000 volunteers. They serve on the Research Ethics Committees, the National Research and Ethics Advisory Panel, the Confidentiality Advisory Group and are part of our patient and public involvement network. All give their time freely to support health and social care research and the HRA's work. They make an invaluable contribution to our work, to research and to research participants.* (Health Research Authority 2019: 6)

The HRA has stated, on its website, that as it protects the interests of patients and the public, it has to understand what these interests are and therefore involves them in order to include their insights (See also Health Research Authority 2018).

Key Questions 4.1
What interests are patients and the public likely to have in a research project to explore the effects on older people awaiting an operation for cancer of increasing the amount they exercise?

4.4   What Is Lay Involvement in Research Ethics?

In the UK all research institutions, not just health research organisations, are required to set up their own procedures for ethical review of research. For example, a university in England has set out the types of members it requires in the terms of reference of its own Research Ethics Committee. These must include a chair and deputy chair who are senior academics; at least one other academic from a university department to provide a 'broad base of research experience and methodological expertise'; at least one lay member; at least one male and one female member; at least one member with experience of managing ethical issues; other individuals seconded with experience or methodological expertise relating to the area of research being reviewed. Not all members of this REC have to be involved in every review and the number of members, quorum, needed to authorise a decision will vary according to the type of ethics review required. So a minimum number of lay members may be required, as in this example, to take part in decisions as equal decision-makers about whether the ethical arrangements in a research study under review are adequate, but the need for experience and expertise may also require more and different types of lay members to be recruited.

Similarly, when arranging to regulate ethics in health research, the HRA's 'Standard Operating Procedures for Research Ethics Committees, June 2019' require at least seven members to attend to be quorate for a meeting with enough of the appropriate types of people to be able to make valid decisions:

> *Subject to paragraph 2.29, the quorum for meetings of a REC is seven members, including at least the following:*
>
> - *The Chair or, if unavailable, the vice-Chair or alternate vice-Chair.*
> - *One lay member (where CTIMPs* [Clinical Trial of an Investigational Medicinal Product] *will be reviewed at the meeting, a lay+ member as defined in the Clinical Trial Regulations must be present for the meeting to be quorate).*
> - *One expert member.* (UK Health Departments Research Ethics Service 2019: 66)

Authentic lay involvement here means lay people having an equal voice with the other committee members, and having appropriate backgrounds to help decide on adequate ethical arrangements. This involves agreeing what needs to be done to protect people taking part in the research being reviewed, based on the experience required of the people who will be selected to take part. Lay members will need to voice their opinions confidently in group discussions to consider ethical arrangements, which can last several hours.

Key Questions 4.2

Where should research ethics committees look to find suitable lay people?

How can they ensure lay people have sufficient experience of the subject to be researched?

How can they ensure that the lay people have the relevant experience of working within committees and the necessary confidence?

Why should research ethics committees offer induction and training to help widen the pool of lay people available?

4.5   What Are the Ethics of Lay Involvement?

We have seen how in the late 1940s there was widespread international support for ensuring health research met ethical responsibilities for protecting and involving the wider community. We also saw how in the 1960s concerns to ensure research was designed and run with appropriate technical and professional scientific expertise reversed at least some of these changes, restricting opportunities for community involvement and leading to debates about power, where it was being concentrated and how it was or was not shared between the various stakeholders (see Chap. 2). Some of those feeling oppressed and also excluded, such as some service user groups, minorities and various dissenters from majority scientific or cultural opinion, have since become more vocal. Nonetheless, the power to actively shape research continues largely to remain more with expert researcher groups and organisations than with community members who could and should also be involved to ensure research is relevant and can be put into practice.

Successfully using patient and public involvement to change the distribution of power has a long way to go. The experiences of those with most control of the processes of making recent changes, from welfare and disability payments to allocating funding for research, often administrators, remain very distant from the experiences of those most affected by such decisions and those seeking to be involved, yet who remain largely excluded (see Beresford 2016).

NHS England offers plenty of detailed, specific guidance on the involvement of approximately three million volunteers (NHS England 2017). The need to provide this and to be clear about what must be done to keep safe volunteers and those they were working with, was reinforced by the Lampard Inquiry into issues relating to Jimmy Saville's widespread abuse of his access as a volunteer (Lampard and Marsden 2015). PPI volunteers are giving their time and understanding specifically to shape and review the research process. However, the links between NHS guidance on safe and appropriate volunteer involvement in health services on the one hand, and the practice of public involvement in general and in health and social care research in particular on the other, are unclear. At times, the latter seems to directly contradict the NHS's own standards of involvement and its own stated ambition. For example, the NIHR Standards of Involvement suggest providing "*clear, concise benchmarks for effective public involvement alongside indicators against which improvement can be monitored*" (NIHR 2018: 2). These Standards are based on specific results from a public consultation. However, if they are to help build relationships and involvement in community practice, they need to provide more specific detail and some clearer concepts, and reasons for adopting them that can engage and be shared with communities that may have been excluded until now. Sharing power in research more equitably and explicitly between researchers, organisations, service users and members of the public may require them to work together to share ideas on *consequences, duties* and *what is good* in research, to provide detailed and ethical guidance and standards to inform PPI in research and in research ethics review (see also Hoddinott et al. 2018).

Such standards cannot be designed as fixed rules, or to provide fixed ideas about public involvement in research. However, they can aid us when working to set realistic expectations of lay members undertaking freely chosen, well-informed and supported roles and moral actions; and encourage improvements in the quality and power of public involvement in research. Over time, such standards can provide organisations with minimum expectations of public involvement in research. You will still need to tailor them to suit your situation, including the type of research you are doing; the resources—money, people and skills—you have available; and your purpose in involving the public in research (NIHR RDS 2014). If we refer back to the three ways of thinking about ethics we met at the beginning of this chapter, we can see that several ethical issues will affect how we can equitably involve PPI members in ethical reviews. Identifying how these apply in research you are involved in will help you reflect on and address power issues in research. Doing this can both ensure you can find ways to balance the power of researchers with the power of the public to shape research topics, and their experiences, including when they are involved in ethical reviews.

The work of RECs is often demanding, technical and tiring. We will therefore need to consider the *consequences* of any measures we take which may lead us to select some types of volunteers rather than others, thus avoiding subjecting people to pressures to take on particular duties, or failing to pay their expenses fairly. Duties that apply to all REC members will include protecting research participants' safety, intellectual property and people's personal information by keeping it confidential. We will also need to make clear what *moral conduct* will be expected of all REC members, including discussing and reporting their work transparently and honestly.

4.6   INCLUSION AND EXCLUSION

We can now more fully appreciate how and why being alert to the issues that relate to including and excluding people from research and from research processes, is almost universally seen as central for designing research to produce findings which can build knowledge about particular groups and populations (Council of Europe 2012). This is underlined as an ethical issue when we want to ensure that research is sensitive and applicable to all the groups or populations that it needs to apply to and is therefore inclusive. However, we may also have noticed in following the journey of this chapter, that it will also be an ethical issue for reviewing research and for RECs, if we are to include every lay or stakeholder group that needs to be taken into account.

Deciding how many people and with what characteristics are to take part in a study will be covered in its research design. The research design will set *inclusion criteria* for how many people of what type to include. In quantitative clinical research, this will be decided by statistical measures used to calculate group sizes needed to represent wider populations. In qualitative research on peoples' views, beliefs and experiences, it will be decided by identifying people likely to be able to provide relevant knowledge. However, there may also be groups defined according to exclusion criteria, who may need to be excluded from the research. This may be because they would be exposed to unacceptable risks of harm specifically related to their situation if included, or because they do not have the language, skills or resources needed to take part in activities or conversations through which the research data is collected, or because they are unable to give informed consent. In some cases, we may need to question how far these are acceptable exclusions, or whether they relate to questions of access which might not arise with the provision of adequate funding for support resources such as interpreters or personal assistants.

Setting out inclusion and exclusion criteria is therefore an important part of preparing to apply for research ethical review of a health or social care study, as well as key to the research design. This is to make sure that people are being appropriately included; that is to say appropriately in terms of being the right types of people in the right numbers to fit the purposes and design of research. It is also concerned with the capabilities of people to play their part in research and to be facilitated to do so by being provided with appropriate information, support and safeguards to take part fully and safely. PPI members of RECs will have the experience and understanding to consider how appropriate these groups and arrangements to safeguard and support them may be. Similarly, exclusion criteria need to be ethically reviewed to ensure that groups are not being excluded for inappropriate reasons. These might be because the research team is failing to be aware of actions which discriminate against particular groups, or because the groups are being devalued or overlooked elsewhere in wider society, perhaps in relation to gender, class or ethnicity. However, appropriate reasons for not including them may relate to people's lack of capacities to give consent or undertake actions required to provide data and/or to be safeguarded within the resources of the planned project.

Exercise 4.2
Research to find out ways to work with people with learning disabilities to enable them to self-manage their healthy eating means that some groups might be included or excluded depending on how differences in spoken and written language abilities are accommodated in research organization and communication. What additional resources might be needed?

4.7   Ethics and Power

For as long as the importance of ethics in the regulation of health services and health research has been recognised worldwide, it has been underpinned by acknowledging that "*participation, transparency, and accountability…, the process by which decisions are made is as important as the outcome of the decisions*" (Coleman et al. 2008: 578). This means that building in genuine community oversight of ethical systems and practice is essential to well-conducted research that can work to safeguard community interests in health and wellbeing. However, as we have seen, for those affected by research to participate equally, it means making research and the terms for taking part in it accountable to and take account of community values, and not just technical research design requirements. This calls for us to work to counter power imbalances between groups in the wider society and in the world of research. Whether this is done or not will also influence how far community-related groups are given information, space, and a say, to prepare them to equitably shape the ethics decisions that matter to differing communities in promoting health and social care research.

Power can be defined as the ability of individuals or groups to get others to do what they want them to do, even when those others do not want to do it. (Iphofen and Poland 1998: 19)

Acting ethically requires people to do the right thing, to work with others constructively, to do what needs to be done to safeguard other people's wellbeing and to include them in decisions about how to do this. This does not happen as a matter of course, but requires people to have the means to change the behaviour of others and to handle disagreements. Making decisions is an act of power and gaining power for PPI members may mean persuading others to share making difficult decisions, including about ethics. But this may also necessitate a struggle as other people may be unwilling to share power or the resources to empower PPI members.

We can act to increase the power of PPI to make a difference in research and research ethics by identifying what resources may be available to PPI members and those wishing to increase their power to do so, and then using those resources to act with impact on others. Relevant resources can be: *economic* such as money or property; *personal* such as ability to work, communicate or share unique knowledge; or *collective* such as social networks, or membership of groups such as service user or disability groups. We can see that while many groups linked to PPI may not have extensive access to economic resources, they may well have access to highly relevant personal and collective resources which other members of research groups or RECs may not have. PPI members may use such resources to exercise political power by offering or withholding them; and all REC members may need to be aware of the different but equivalent political resources available to all members, including PPI members, to support their presence and contributions to ethical review.

4.8   IDENTIFYING AND DECIDING ETHICAL ISSUES
IN PRACTICE

When we take part in ethical reviews of particular research projects, we can use the ideas and knowledge of legal duties and social expectations which we have examined here, to decide what we can do to identify ethical issues and then decide which of them need to be addressed and what PPI can and should contribute. See Table 4.1 for key initial questions to ask.

This shows that if we are to ensure that relevant ethical issues are considered as fully as possible, this means taking into account diverse

Table 4.1 Identifying and deciding ethical issues in practice: key questions to ask

- What actions are being planned, and what effects may they have on the freedoms, safety and welfare of people being asked to take part?
- Are there aspects of the abilities and situation of individuals or groups being asked to take part which lay them open to particular harms or benefits, or put at risk or enhance their ability to give their informed consent?
- Have the research project team provided enough information to enable PPI members to identify the relevant ethical issues, and to be confident that they have put in place measures to address them and have the expertise to do so?
- Have the research team adequately involved PPI members and lay groups to give them the knowledge and understanding of what the ethical issues are, the means of managing them, and their relevance?
- What means of managing the ethical issues should be considered and has the research project team appropriately said what these should be?
- Are PPI members able to express their viewpoints on the ethical issues at stake about which they are best informed to make judgments and their effects on particular groups?
- Are PPI members able to listen to and understand the viewpoints of others involved in the ethical discussion to decide what is the best reasonable course of action and whether the particular project they are considering is offering the best reasonable course of action?
- When reaching an overall review decision on whether a project's design has met its ethical obligations, have all committee members been able to judge and agree its ethical consequences, who will benefit most and whether people's rights will be safeguarded if the design is put into practice?
- Will the planned project have outcomes which could benefit the wider community?
- Will the planned project treat participants with equal respect?
- Are PPI members able to review the results of the ethics decision they have contributed to?
- After seeing what these are, how will PPI members judge the consequences of what that ethics decision was and what they were able to contribute to it?
- Are PPI members content they made the contribution they needed to fulfil their responsibilities as a PPI member?
- Overall, would PPI members judge the effects of the review process as beneficial or harmful to individuals or the wider community?

viewpoints, and ensuring they are managed appropriately every time ethics comes up for review. This section has summarised the key questions for PPI members to bear in mind if they are to take an active part in making such decisions. This whole chapter has set out how there is a basis in law and in professional and social practice for asking such questions and offered ways of supporting PPI members to have the confidence and power to do so.

4.9   SUMMARY AND CONCLUSIONS

We need to consider ethics as the most basic requirement to take into account when we plan and carry out research. The law is used to strictly regulate and formalise how these requirements must be met. These requirements extend to research needing to be demonstrably of adequate quality, likely to produce effective findings of community benefit, and to protect people from harms in the course of developing and realising all aspects of the research. As well as the legal and professional ethical requirements, we have also recognised that the relevance and applicability of community issues and viewpoints need to be considered, and PPI contributions can modify and amplify these. Most importantly, we can see why good patient and public involvement is essential to our ability to adequately recognise what words, discussions, methods and actions are appropriate to address ethical considerations which arise from any research we review in terms of those it is likely to affect.

REFERENCES

Beresford, P. (2016). *All our welfare: Towards participatory social policy*. Bristol: Policy Press.

Coleman, C. H., Bouësseau, M. C., & Reis, A. (2008). The contribution of ethics to public health. *Bulletin of the World Health Organization, 86*, 577–578.

Coleman, C., Lemmens, T., Mehra, T., Toure, A., & Bouësseau, M. C. (2009). *Research ethics committees: Basic concepts for capacity-building*. Geneva: WHO.

Council of Europe. (2012). *Guide for research ethics committee members: Steering committee on bioethics*. Council of Europe.

Health Research Authority. (2018). *Governance arrangements for research ethics committees: 2018 edition*. London: Department of Health & Social Care.

Health Research Authority. (2019). *Health Research Authority annual report and accounts 2018/19*. NHS Health Research Authority.

Hoddinott, P., Pollock, A., O'Cathain, A., Boyer, I., Taylor, J., MacDonald, C., Oliver, S., & Donovan, J. L. (2018). How to incorporate patient and public perspectives into the design and conduct of research. *F1000Research, 7*, 752. https://doi.org/10.12688/f1000research.15162.1.

Hunt, P. (1981). Settling accounts with the parasite people: A critique of 'A life apart' by E.J Miller and G.V. Gwynne. *Disability Challenge, 1*, 37–50.

Iphofen, R., & Poland, F. (1998). *Sociology in practice for health care professionals*. Hampshire: Macmillan Press.

Kaptein, M., & Wempe, J. (2002). Three general theories of ethics and the integrative role of integrity theory. *SSRN Electronic Journal*. https://doi.org/10.2139/ssrn.1940393.

Lampard, K., & Marsden, E. (2015). *Themes and lessons learnt from NHS investigations into matters relating to Jimmy Savile: Independent report for the Secretary of State for Health* (no place).

Maori Health Committee of the Health Research Council of New Zealand. (2010). *Guidelines for researchers on health research involving Maori' version 2.* Health Research Council of New Zealand.

Miller, E. J., & Gwynne, G. V. (1972). *A life apart*. London: Tavistock.

NHS England. (2017). *Recruiting and managing volunteers in NHS providers, a practical guide*. NHS England.

NIHR. (2018). *National standards for public involvement in research*. London: NIHR.

NIHR RDS. (approx 2014). *Patient and public involvement in health and social care research: A handbook for researchers*. London: NIHR RDS.

The National Health and Medical Research Council, the Australian Research Council and Universities Australia. (Updated 2018). *National statement on ethical conduct in human research 2007*. Canberra: Commonwealth of Australia.

UK Health Departments Research Ethics Service. (2019). *Standard operating procedures for research ethics committees*. Health Research Authority.

CHAPTER 5

Critical Perspectives on Patient and Public Involvement in Research

Perhaps unexpectedly for some, this book does not skate over difficulties and tensions that can arise through involvement. Instead, we explain how collaboration can be better when we recognise that making new partnerships can be disruptive, especially if existing practices exclude some people who may want to be included, and that changes may be resisted. We have therefore considered how, in building good PPI, we may need to make, hear and use criticism to good and constructive effect.

> PPI operates as an empty signifier, intermittently populated with whatever policy ideas of citizen engagement are a la mode (Stewart 2012). Maynard (2012) depicts contemporary health policy making as Nirvania, a land of faith inhabited by zombies and unicorns. (Madden and Speed 2017: 5)

This almost poetic assertion by Madden and Speed (2017) referring to Stewart (2012), and Maynard (2012) suggests that even after several decades of different types of PPI activity and their reported benefits, there is little shared agreement on the aims and rationale for PPI, what it does, how well it is working or what its impact is. This is despite extensive discussions with and guidance to stakeholders, research communities, health and social care services and PPI volunteers. We may blame such confusion on the lack of strong concepts to underpin and envisage PPI (Locock et al. 2017). However, as earlier chapters have shown, conceptualising PPI may not be simple, as the concepts different people bring to PPI practice have emerged from and are tied to complex histories and motivations both for

© The Author(s) 2020
J. Grotz et al., *Patient and Public Involvement in Health and Social Care Research*, https://doi.org/10.1007/978-3-030-55289-3_5

developing and promoting PPI and for being involved in it. Adopting a selective approach, which addresses just some of the concepts which are current but overlooks or dismisses others, will give rise to criticisms from some groups and organisations of what has been happening in PPI, and of the ideas of some others which are currently shaping PPI practice. Instead we look at some of the main criticisms of PPI features, how and why they are raised and who is raising them. This will help us to think about how we can use them to strengthen our ideas about what concepts and practices we may want to prioritise in order to improve PPI in our own activities or more widely.

Over the whole time that patient and public involvement has been promoted and developed, its many forms have been criticised for reasons across a spectrum of viewpoints. Here we have divided them into three simple, broad categories:

- Firstly, some academics suggest that PPI activities and concerns infringe their academic freedom to produce independent ideas and evidence. They therefore call into question the place and value of PPI in research and describe it as an unnecessary bureaucratic burden.
- Secondly, many long-standing campaigners for service user rights see PPI as only window-dressing. According to this view, PPI is continuing to deny rather than increase the access service users seek in order to produce and own knowledge so that they can shape services to better fit their needs or interests.
- Finally, the most widespread current criticism raised in PPI, researcher and other stakeholder groupings concerns how PPI is being implemented in practice, often presenting it as a half-hearted tick box exercise that meets a formal requirement.

All of these largely reflect Matthews' observations that there is not yet a widespread commitment to fully embed PPI in research practice (Matthews et al. 2019).

The first two categories of criticism reflect two polarised and persistent standpoints about what the purposes of research are, how it should be organised and whether moral as well as scientific principles should inform research planning. They can be described as an 'us and them' approach.

The first standpoint sees research as best carried out based on objective scientific principles and therefore by science experts. It presents the moral views and values of PPI participants in general, and campaigning groups in particular, as likely to undermine rather than enhance high-quality research findings. This standpoint places priority on eliminating any interests in research which these academics see as being extraneous and introducing bias, and which will therefore distort and weaken robust research designs. Criticisms of PPI from this standpoint define it as a source of bias which needs to be seen as a barrier, rather than helpful to good research, where good research is defined as objective research.

The second standpoint sees research and research implementation as an activity which depends on public support, and therefore needs to clearly demonstrate how it contributes to the public good. Based on this view, research needs to be organised in such a way that it is overseen by appropriately informed members of the public who need to be able to judge for themselves what is good for the wider society. Criticisms of PPI from this standpoint define it as being excessively controlled by a system made up of health professionals, which makes PPI anti-democratic; as exclusive rather than inclusive; and as protecting the dominant position of bio-medical professions to judge what is good, even when they claim to be involving patients and the public.

These overarching adversarial arguments often hide great complexity; within each standpoint there can be further divisions and contests. For example, people can disagree about who offers the most authentic voice. Some service users have rejected the suggestion that the large national charities can genuinely represent them when they are run by paid employees who are recruited for qualities or skills other than those gained through the sustained and direct lived experiences shared by service users (Branfield et al. 2006: 20).

The third category of criticisms focuses on reasons why PPI is so often implemented in practice in a way that is superficial rather than comprehensively embraced. This may be for any number of reasons from not introducing PPI at a sufficiently early stage in the research to not having sufficient PPI members on the research team, not selecting people with the relevant lived experience, or involving people with whom the researchers are already familiar rather than seeking new voices.

What all these categories of criticism have in common is that they are not simply based on logical argument but reflect values that inform judgements about what should happen, and will therefore attach blame to some groups if they act in a different way to the approach they themselves advocate.

There are further reasons for disagreement between researchers since there are also different types of research. These range from medical research, which tests the effects of clinical treatment and may therefore lay particular emphasis on ensuring findings are objective, to research on the way in which services are delivered, which may sometimes need to take into account subjective experiences and views on the manner, and the emotional and cultural appropriateness of service delivery.

There are also different types of PPI, which can be formally supported by organisations and which we question later in this chapter, which may reflect campaigns by pressure groups or be generated by individuals presenting particular under-recognised experiences.

Understanding these varying perspectives helps us to see how there can be such divergent views as to whether policy initiatives relating to PPI based on research have real value. Some observers such as Barnes and Mercer (1997) have seen developing statutory requirements as an important step towards ensuring changes can be more widely implemented so as to meet the demands of service users to shape both research programmes and the services they aim to inform. However, other commentators, such as Tritter and Koivusalo (2013), see formal policies as too often marking a step backwards because of the terms and language they use which:

> *undermines the principle of patient and public involvement, public accountability and returns the power for prioritisation of health services to an unaccountable medical elite.* (ibid: 115)

To better understand the reasons for these different views and to decide which ones may actually help improve PPI contributions to research, we now look more specifically at the questions they raise:

- Do we need academic freedom in research?
- What is a service user perspective?
- What are potentially negative impacts of PPI?
- Can we agree on how to evaluate PPI?

5.1   Do We Need Academic Freedom in Research?

The ideal of academic freedom supported by some academics suggests that it is desirable, and possible, to regulate access to the process of creating knowledge so as to ensure that it is equitable, unbiased and free from unreasonable interference from people who may be judged to be acting in their own interests. Five key areas of action for ensuring freedom from bias in the research process, especially in studies of clinical developments, are: choosing topics; defining study questions; research design; data analysis and, last but not least, allocating funding. If research results were to be produced without examining the possibility of bias in these areas, this would undermine the scientific status of specific types of findings, such as whether newly developed treatments are effective. An example of the kinds of conflict of interest that involving patient or public groups may bring is where they are committed in some way to a particular outcome in advance. For instance, in a case where patients suffering from myalgic encephalomyelitis (ME), a condition that causes extreme tiredness, had seen the loss of a consultant post in their local health service, they and their carers set up a pressure group to try to ensure that any report with recommendations on a new service must recommend reinstating the consultant post. Promoting this standpoint would pre-empt whatever evidence was to be collected and examined in such a report.

There are ways of overcoming this problem by the selection of a balanced group of PPI members rather than focusing on a single pressure group; the initial conversation with PPI members when motivations are discussed; and the allocation of roles, along with training for researchers to make them aware of potential problems.

While codes of practice for academic researchers regularly require any financial interests to be disclosed, patient groups may receive funding from a variety of sources that they are not routinely required to disclose. These sources may range from fund-raising themselves to support from local authorities, hospitals and local or national charities, or even pharmaceutical companies. That patient organisations can have such financial interests which are not disclosed has been evidenced recently by research such as Mandeville et al. (2019). This study showed how patient organisations could quite commonly have financial interests such as funds from pharmaceutical companies, which were not routinely covered by disclosure policies, even when the organisations were involved in assessments of health technologies. The study covered patient organisations, which might be charities or voluntary organisations, with incomes ranging from less than £20,000 (€22,000; $25,000) to more than £119 million (€133 million; $144 million) and where *"The percentage of their pharmaceutical industry funding ranged from less than 1% to one organisation deriving nearly 70% of its income from three manufacturers"* (ibid: 4). Patient organisations receiving substantial funds linked with such industries may be expected to have some constraints on their freedom to express concerns or criticisms relating to them. This concern about bias could be resolved if PPI participants and the groups to which they belong were required to submit a declaration of their personal and financial interests as are medical research groups. Requiring such declarations is a common practice in the NHS and local government, where all members of strategic and decision-making boards, both staff and lay representatives, are required to submit this type of declaration.

UK law, in common with that of several other developed countries on various continents, protects academics who want to research unconventional or controversial topics in new ways and to publish unpopular opinions, so that they are free to rigorously test findings.

> *academic staff have freedom within the law to question and test received wisdom, and to put forward new ideas and controversial or unpopular opinions, without placing themselves in jeopardy of losing their jobs or privileges they may have at their institutions.* (Education Reform Act 1988, para 202: 194)

This UK legislation was designed to address concerns about the way research is supported, including how funding is allocated. However, it does raise the question as to whether such principles should extend to PPI, especially if PPI participants are to be included in bodies with the power to veto or reject research funding. Does the requirement to include patients and the public in such work infringe on this right to academic freedom? Some academics argue that this freedom allows them to restrict patient and public involvement, for example, if research involves animal experiments where public opinion is sharply divided (see Animals (Scientific Procedures) Act 1986).

While we have not found examples of PPI involvement leading directly to academics not being able to undertake research, it is the case in the UK that the absence of suitable PPI in applications has been given as a reason for rejecting applications for research funding. In Case Example 5: Funding Criteria, we provide an example where a funding organisation made it explicit that funding would not be allocated to a study if researchers remained in sole control with overall power to direct the research. Indeed, it also required the applicant, a charitable organisation, which was leading and responsible for delivering the research programme, to provide evidence within the application that it was representative of its community too.

Case Example 5 Funding Criteria
National Lottery Charities Board Research Grants Programme
In the early 2000s the newly established National Lottery Charities Board ran a research grants programme funding charities to undertake high quality research, often in collaboration with universities. Two of the key published assessment criteria were:

- "The applicant organisation is leading the research project and has the capacity to maintain this role".
- "The applicant organisation is representative of its community and the research project and organisation have appropriate beneficiary involvement".

This meant that university research departments could not be in sole control and if organisations and research partners could not adequately address these two criteria, applications were likely to be rejected, even if the research proposal received high scores in other criteria of the expert assessments such as appropriateness of methodology or skills of named researchers.
(Application pack: Research Grants Programme: Funding medical and social research, Community Fund – operating name of the National Lottery Charities Board)

We therefore argue that there are many complexities underlying both the ideas of academic freedom and also the idea that PPI necessarily provides an independent voice in research. If either academic researchers or PPI groups are dependent on receiving funding or support from any other source, they could be seen as being beholden to some extent to the bodies which provide that support and therefore not wholly independent. This makes it especially important that, when taking part in decision-making about any aspect of research, including allocating research funding, those taking part in such decisions should disclose such interests. This enables other people to judge what other influences, or biases, may have come into play in taking decisions and in producing results. Arguing the case for academic freedom implies a principled critique of PPI member involvement in research to determine whether it is too close to the research topic, and thus biased, to produce good research results. This would make PPI at best an unnecessary burden to research through the need to determine the closeness of PPI members to the research topic, and at worst an approach which intrinsically undermines good research.

The next section looks more closely at arguments for taking into account non-academic perspectives because of the need to add to the kinds of knowledge that academic researchers working alone can provide if it is to be more complete and provide an adequate picture of the research topic. The starting point of this next section is to identify what a service user perspective is and, therefore, what it can add.

5.2   What Is a Service User Perspective?

The idea and presence of a distinctive service user perspective in the UK can be traced back over many years to at least the 1970s (Beresford 2013). The calls for this perspective to be recognised have been translated in a variety of ways into the governance and practice of research in many countries (Barnes and Mercer 1997; Richards 2017).

The arguments for the need to pay attention to service user perspectives are in many ways the mirror image of the arguments for academic freedom. The arguments for academic freedom are that being too close to the research topic weakens the independence of the research process and results. In contrast, the arguments for taking into account service user perspectives are that omitting the views and experience of the public and service users will overlook an essential and authentic part of the area of study in terms of evidence, context and relevance, and that this would weaken the value of the research findings.

We have seen that service user perspectives are diverse and complex and that individual service users can often prefer to speak for themselves. However, some of the key arguments can be summarised and examined in terms of what difference they might make to common assumptions in the research community about how research should be carried out. We have seen that service users can often experience being excluded in a general sense from decisions about the way in which the services they receive are provided, and also from the production of that knowledge which is directly relevant to enabling them to understand and assess the services they receive. They may also see themselves as being excluded from the discussions about why, how and when they are excluded. The arguments for the need to safeguard and exercise academic freedom as it will provide more objective evidence can be used to justify such exclusion precisely because the experience, interests and focus of academics are disconnected from service users' concerns. In contrast, the arguments for including a service user perspective are that their experience, interests and focus provide distinctive, complementary and essential ingredients to well-founded, relevant research.

Debates which suggest that service user perspectives are needed to provide better evidence and more realistic ways of implementing research also call into question assumptions that service users do not need to be able to speak for themselves but can be represented by clinical or health or social care professionals in discussions about what services they receive or what the research evidence is saying about the need for or the effectiveness of such services. These professionals are in fact a distinct group who we would expect researchers to speak to in gathering evidence relating to the research topic; they will contribute information about the practicalities of delivering services as well as their effects. Representatives of the professionals may be members of advisory groups.

In addition, such assumptions about service users may unreasonably underestimate their capacity and knowledge to judge the quality of services and how appropriate they are to their own circumstances compared with those of health or social care professionals. The debates may also overlook the stark reality that services often offer little power to service users to influence the processes which shape them (Beresford and Wilson 1998: 89).

Service users increasingly call for the process of producing knowledge to be well understood and recognised as a process in which knowledge is actually and necessarily co-produced with them, and that it will be incomplete if all the views and voices of relevant groups are not actively recognised as part of that process. Early chapters in this book have aimed to follow the example of Beresford (2019) by putting this debate into its 'historical, theoretical and philosophical context' to show how public and service user perspectives have been present and constantly developing over a long period of time, even when given less prominence. As power, politics, policies and ideas about judging high-quality research have changed over time, so the extent to which service user perspectives have been acknowledged to even exist or at least be legitimate have varied greatly. However, if, as Beresford (2019) suggests, there is now wider agreement that co-produced research produces more complete knowledge, then this provides good grounds to call for more equal access to research funding for co-produced research studies, especially those co-produced with user-led organisations.

This discussion raises the question of the effects of more, or wider, inclusion. It may favour service users with better connections to mainstream or majority groups in the wider population at the expense of ordinary service users. This could remove power and influence from groups who see themselves as disenfranchised and who continue to challenge the mainstream and its dominant systems. If this is the case, important contributions that counterbalance academic or professional assumptions may again be overlooked.

To take this argument a step further, there is a need to balance this wider inclusion with retaining the focus on lived experience. Individuals or groups who are involved at the forefront of inclusive developments may feel that resources should be focused on the area in which they are particularly interested rather than others; they may in fact have very special interests. In highlighting their own different positions and interests, such a group may question whether moving towards the widest possible democratic involvement and adopting a consensus could adversely affect and drown out their call for recognising a specific case on which they wish to express their views. They may feel more comfortable with clinical or care professionals with specialist knowledge speaking on their behalf or adding their views, but would be concerned if others without their lived experience or technical knowledge were to end up speaking for them. This could be the case if the people with special interests were seen as a pressure group. Here researchers may too readily assume that because these 'other groups' are neither academics nor professionals, they may be taken to speak legitimately for those who have experience of the research topic. In the case we mentioned earlier of patients with ME, different patient support groups have very different views about what is appropriate and acceptable clinical treatment and support and it cannot be taken for granted that any lay group, nor any professional group, would fully appreciate and represent these diverse views.

We began with the question 'What is a service user perspective?' and have established both that service user groups may well have experiences and priorities that are different from those shared by many academic and professional groups and sometimes other patient and public groups. We have also seen that the criticisms of research processes and findings as being 'too disconnected' from the reality of services have been to some extent conceded by many publicly funded, charitable and government organisations. However, it does not yet seem possible to establish a representative model of a single unified service user perspective distinct from academic and professional perspectives. This is particularly the case if we want to retain the advantages of ensuring that we continue to be open to and distinctively reflect changes in society, social groupings and ideas about health, illness and good treatment while also working to increase access to information and the ability to share all this through social media. This means that there will always be more and novel emerging sources of criticisms of research and of research communities from the public, and from service users, particularly those members experiencing exclusion. It also means that there can be no permanent and static system for representing all types of service user perspective, as these will also be emerging from changing populations, and service developments. We therefore need to remain aware of the need to constantly review how we can deal more effectively with the exclusions and omissions identified when we examine and continue to focus on service user perspectives.

Exercise 5.1
Who should be included as PPI members in a study of technological support for children with cerebral palsy?

So far, we have considered the main positive arguments for recognising and including both academic and public and service user views and involvement. In the next section, we look in more detail at criticisms of PPI which take into account the evidence that PPI may have negative as well as positive impacts.

5.3   WHAT ARE POTENTIALLY NEGATIVE IMPACTS OF PPI?

In Chap. 3 (Sect. 3.6) we addressed the question of how to prepare to deal with things that go wrong in the course of PPI because we know that, at times, things will go wrong. In this section, we examine what impact that may have. If we are to do so, we need to think more about the reasons why things go wrong. Criticisms of PPI in these circumstances are less criticisms of the principles governing PPI, which we have examined in the previous two sections of this chapter but criticisms directed more at what happens when PPI is being undertaken for the wrong reasons. These can include: nobody has taken the time to identify and spell out what a good PPI contribution in relation to the project in hand should look like; information may have been used or shared which was wrong, perhaps it was inaccurate or was not appropriate to this project or its particular participants; perhaps involvement was being carried out without due care for matching and supporting the people and practices involved; or perhaps confidential information was shared outside the project. In any of these circumstances, being involved in PPI can actually negatively affect the health and wellbeing of PPI members, can waste precious project resources and can negatively affect research outcomes. Having considered the ethical issue in Chap. 4, we can recognise all of these possibilities as posing serious ethical risks. In some cases, it may mean that the project does not even get off the ground because PPI arrangements required by the project design, by funders or sponsors cannot be set up, or because the quality of engagement with participants is not good enough to recruit and retain them. In all of these cases, there can be a wide range of reasons for failure or for negative impacts. Reasons can commonly include poor practice in planning or supporting PPI, which in turn can be caused by lack of training for researchers who will work with PPI members, or lack of resources available to research organisers. They can also include bad judgements made by PPI members, which again may be caused by lack of training or support for them so that they are unable to fully understand the scope and demands of the PPI role in the project to which they are contributing. Firm evidence of the type and extent of such negative impacts is difficult to find as for several reasons it rarely gets reported. In Case Example 6: The failed symposium on collaboration and inclusion, we provide an example from a learning event for research partners led by the author JG and experienced by co-author FP.

Case Example 6   The failed symposium on collaboration and inclusion
In 2006 I organised a symposium about collaborative practice in inclusive research. It didn't go well. The symposium had set out to clarify the concept of collaborative practices, to identify their purpose, to recognise the needs of the partners, to identify how quality could be ensured, and finally to ask the question when and how it would be known if collaborative practice was working.

I had tried to follow best practice guidelines and arranged for 19 participants bringing service providers, academics and service users with widely varying access needs to take part, providing support for those diverse access needs. During the symposium, three distinct perspectives were expressed: the principled, the pragmatic and the personal. The principled perspective appeared to arise mostly from rejecting any set definition of 'inclusive research'. This decision led to dropping the term 'inclusive' altogether and effectively ended the discussion. In contrast, the pragmatic perspectives provided a range of reasons for continuing to collaborate. The personal perspectives particularly raised the question of why service users would wish to participate in the research process at all.

In the event participants could not agree on any single clear purpose for collaborative practice in inclusive research and evaluated the event as not having provided useful findings.

From Grotz, 'collaborative practice in research, a bridge too far?' A presentation at the 13th VSSN / NCVO "Researching the Voluntary Sector" Conference, 5th–6th September 2007.

We suggest that key lessons from this 'failed symposium' were about how important it was to co-produce ground rules and resources to enable all participants, including service users, to discuss topics in terms and for purposes they saw as comfortable and useful for them.

A further criticism relating to PPI may be that there are not enough recorded examples of negative impacts of PPI for people to reliably understand how to make it as effective as possible with everybody fully engaged. We argue that it will be important for PPI members and researchers to make more time to attend to, record and share lessons from negative outcomes of PPI activities they have been involved in. A study examining the ethical implications of participatory research worldwide (Beier et al. 2019) has argued that sufficient time, rigour and resources are needed for patients or citizens to be truly involved in the kinds of deliberation which are essential to safeguard participants and also produce research results that the public can trust. They report that patients with the condition Amyotrophic Lateral Sclerosis (ALS) organised themselves as co-investigators to take lithium to contradict the results of a smaller research study because they believed that this could benefit the condition. However, the authors argue that if trials initiated by patients are not safeguarded by traditional research ethics, the participants may run serious risks and we know that terminally ill patients may be more prepared to face significant levels of risk in the hopes of securing positive individual outcomes and research findings. Achieving adequate learning from negative as well as positive effects of PPI will therefore depend in part on the research organisers creating a culture of openness, transparency and trust within their project. Learning from negative as well as positive outcomes of PPI can help all of us to reflect on our responsibilities to make PPI experiences as positive and as useful as possible. However, there are many pressures from funders, sponsors and publishers to report mainly positive outcomes, which makes it more difficult to openly report negative outcomes and therefore to share knowledge about them.

Exercise 5.2
How can we promote trustful discussion about evaluating a study of self-management of activity by ME patients?

Evaluating PPI activities can help us build our evidence of what contributes to positive and negative PPI experiences from a range of stakeholder viewpoints. We look at some critical issues in evaluating PPI in the next section.

5.4   Can We Agree on How to Evaluate PPI?

An important criticism repeatedly voiced and directed at PPI relates to the lack of evidence to show what difference PPI makes. In an editorial for the British Medical Journal, Boivin et al. (2018) highlighted, in particular, the continuing need to evaluate patient and public involvement in research, attending to the specific values and qualities that make for good quality PPI relationships and distinctive contributions. As key principles, they suggested "*Clarity, Reflexivity, Methodological rigour, Transparency, Pragmatism [and] Reciprocity*" (ibid: 1).

The appearance of this call in a prominent medical research journal underlines the extent to which such evaluation is not currently common. To evaluate how well PPI is working, there needs to be some agreed basis for comparing what people think should be happening in a research study, such as aims and quality criteria; what was happening before the PPI activities, the baseline; and what differences have been made during and since PPI activities, analysis and outcomes. Boivin et al. (2018) have identified the need for *clarity* in terms and aims; for *reflexive* skills in reflecting on one's own and others' activities; for methods used to be devised and applied with *rigour;* for the findings of the evaluation to be recorded and discussed openly and *transparently;* for planned actions to reflect circumstances *pragmatically* and not to apply rigid standards or criteria; and for support to be provided for relationships to be *reciprocal* and therefore equitable and respectful, not one-way.

As we have seen throughout this book, the issues in PPI history and practice have been continually and hotly debated both between different stakeholders in research and also between different PPI groups. This means that in many areas there is no ready-made basis for clarity or consistency in how to undertake such evaluation. Yet unless we can provide more evaluation of what PPI does and how, PPI involvement will continue to be left open to continuing criticisms, which, again, may reflect speculation rather than any systematic observation either of real achievements and progress or of evidenced problems in PPI practice.

> *Uncertainty persists about why and how to do involvement well and evaluate its impact, how to involve and support a diversity of individuals, and in ways that allow them to work in partnership to genuinely influence decision-making. This exposes patient and public involvement (PPI) to criticisms of exclusivity and tokenism.* (Ocloo and Matthews 2016: 626)

The difficulties in evaluating PPI are related directly to the findings of Matthews et al. (2019) in their study of PPI strategy documents that the rationale for PPI remains, in many ways, confused. The absence of a clear shared understanding of what PPI is meant to achieve makes it impossible to readily assess through any evaluation whether it has achieved what it set out to. This lack of clarity is further compounded when we want to compare what evaluations have found in different projects, where different projects may have built in different purposes and expectations for PPI.

We do not seek to attribute fault for the uncertainties arising from the complex challenges of evaluating PPI to any individuals or groups who design or take part in it. We do recognise, however, that there are some particular challenges intrinsic in the praiseworthy innovative directions and intentions which PPI activities have been offering, involving the great efforts and energies of many people. In taking active steps and in working hard to be inclusive and diverse, PPI is moving our system of research practices and understandings away from traditional practices, which gave only researchers power, and expected them to organise research systems and processes alone. However, although the journey towards expecting and developing shared ideas and practices is very much under way, its goal is still a long way from being achieved. We argue that to develop a tailored framework to help us evaluate the dynamic complexities of PPI, we have to pay attention to the wider system of research within which PPI is emerging, as well as to the individual projects within which PPI activities emerge and are carried out. In all of these recognising the importance of critical discussion and taking account of what it tells us has been and will be essential to working towards such a framework.

> *Key Questions 5.1*
> What kind of research project might need to ensure that moral views and values are considered with appropriate patient and public involvement?

We provide some advice on evaluating PPI in projects in Chap. 6 where we link to guides such as "Evaluation: what to consider" (Health Foundation 2015) working within a suggested model for building PPI flexibly, responsively and equitably.

5.5   Summary and Conclusions

In this chapter we have identified the many critical views of both principles and practices in PPI, and provided reasons for them. We have argued that doing this can help us understand why, so often, discussions of PPI can be polarised, and too readily exclude the viewpoints of some groups, whether researchers, professionals, or PPI or service user groups. Yet the ideals for PPI suggest we need to be more rather than less inclusive. If there is a widely shared perception that we do not yet really know whether PPI actually makes a positive difference, we may be tempted to ask whether all the hard work is worth it. We do know that the discussions and activities of current PPI practice have made it possible to think seriously about 'Patients as partners' in research (Seale 2016). King's Fund research in the UK has shown this idea as engaging with the political and conceptual momentum now given to disrupting the 'us and them' dynamic. Taking this discursive stance may well be as relevant for considering the criticisms of PPI as it is for helping us to constructively appreciate the creative and dynamic context of diverse ideas and needs, which must include critical and negative aspects, and which, in turn has shaped and enriched PPI. The next chapter will build a means for us to apply to PPI plans and practice based on the diverse range of historical, practical, ethical and conceptual insights about PPI which we have examined so far.

References

Animals (Scientific Procedures) Act. (1986). Her Majesty's Stationary Office, London.

Barnes, C., & Mercer, G. (1997). *Doing disability research*. Leeds: Disability Press.

Beier, K., Schweda, M., & Schicktanz, S. (2019). Taking patient involvement seriously: A critical ethical analysis of participatory approaches in data-intensive medical research. *BMC Medical Informatics and Decision Making, 19*, 90.

Beresford, P. (2013). From 'other' to involved: User involvement in research: An emerging paradigm. *Nordic Social Work Research, 3*(2), 139–148.

Beresford, P. (2019). Public participation in health and social care: Exploring the co-production of knowledge. *Frontiers in Sociology, 3*, Article 41.

Beresford, P., & Wilson, A. (1998). Social exclusion and social work: Challenging the contradictions of exclusive debate. In M. Barry & C. Hallett (Eds.), *On the margins: Social exclusion and social work − Issues of theory, policy and practice* (pp. 85–96). Dorset: Russell House.

Boivin, A., Richards, T., Forsythe, L., Grégoire, A., L'Espérance, A., Abelson, J., & Carman, K. L. (2018). Evaluating patient and public involvement in research: If we are serious about involvement, we need to be equally serious about evaluation. *BMJ, 363*, k5147. https://doi.org/10.1136/bmj.k5147.

Branfield, F., Beresford, P., Andrews, E. J., Chambers, P., Staddon, P., Wise, G., & Williams-Findlay, B. (2006). *Making user involvement work*. York: Joseph Rowntree Foundation.

Education Reform Act. (1988). Her Majesty's Stationary Office, London.

Health Foundation. (2015). *Evaluation: What to consider*. London: Health Foundation.

Locock, L., Boylan, A. M., Snow, R., & Staniszewska, S. (2017). The power of symbolic capital in patient and public involvement in health research. *Health Expectations, 20*, 836–844.

Madden, M., & Speed, E. (2017). Beware zombies and unicorns: Toward critical patient and public involvement in health research in a neoliberal context. *Frontiers in Sociology, 2*, Article 7.

Mandeville, K. L., Barker, R., Packham, A., Sowerby, C., Yarrow, K., & Patrick, H. (2019). Financial interests of patient organisations contributing to technology assessment at England's National Institute for Health and Care Excellence: policy review. *BMJ, 364*, k5300.

Matthews, R., Kaur, M., French, C., Baker, A., & Reed, J. (2019). How helpful are patient and public involvement strategic documents – Results of a framework analysis using 4Pi National Involvement Standards. *Research Involvement and Engagement, 5*, 31.

Maynard, A. (2012). The Maynard doctrine: The chronicles of Nirvania, home of unicorns and zombies. *Health Policy Insight*. Available at https://www.health-policyinsight.com/?q=node/1433

Ocloo, J., & Matthews, R. (2016). From tokenism to empowerment: Progressing patient and public involvement in healthcare improvement. *BMJ Quality and Safety, 25*(8), 626–632.

Richards, T. (2017). *Patient and public involvement in research goes global*. thebmjopinion. Available at: https://blogs.bmj.com/bmj/2017/11/30/tessa-richards-patient-and-public-involvement-in-research-goes-global/

Seale, B. (2016). *Patients as partners: Building collaborative relationships among professionals, patients, carers and communities*. London: King's Fund.

Stewart, E. (2012). *Governance, participation and avoidance: Everyday public involvement in the Scottish NHS*. Edinburgh: University of Edinburgh.

Tritter, J. Q., & Koivusalo, M. (2013). Undermining patient and public engagement and limiting its impact: The consequences of the health and social care act 2012 on collective patient and public involvement. *Health Expectations, 16*, 115–118.

CHAPTER 6

The Coherence Model

The previous chapters have shown that patient and public involvement (PPI) in research is not just a process of involving people but about constantly changing relationships between people based on whether or not they are involved, and, if they are, in what ways and to what extent. Chapter 1 explained how, if both researchers and lay people are to act differently if they are to become involved, they need to take personal responsibility for their own actions and to understand and be comfortable with their role in the relationships that being involved brings. Chapter 2 described how, over more than a century, such relationships have been changing, what has brought these changes about and what effects that has had on the nature and quality of involvement. Chapter 3 explained reasons for the complexities of those relationships in a research context based on differing ideas, concerns and practicalities. Chapter 4 showed how conducting such relationships raises legal, professional and most importantly ethical requirements and the need to negotiate them. Chapter 5 suggested how overcoming the 'us and them' dynamic is central to involvement and is vital for achieving involvement within what is a complex network of often-opposing critical views.

This chapter will seek to combine all of this knowledge of and insights into involvement by organising them into a road map, a conceptual framework, to which we can refer in planning a type of PPI involvement which will work transparently. Doing this can help us to see that building PPI must be based on understanding the relationships within the following

J. Grotz et al., *Patient and Public Involvement in Health and Social Care Research*, https://doi.org/10.1007/978-3-030-55289-3_6

three elements of a research project. This may start with a first meeting and researchers and PPI participants getting to know each other, *connecting*; then move on to undertaking activities together, *collaborating*, including developing findings and disseminating them; and finally identifying PPI activities that contribute something additional and distinctive that fits in with and adds to the quality of the whole project or experience, *complementing*. We set out this conceptual framework in what we are calling the COHERENCE Model because it enables us to bring together the thinking and actions in the three elements from across our research described above and link them together into a sequence. This is a circular model like the research cycle in Fig. 3.1. This chapter will address these three elements of the COHERENCE Model:

- Connecting
- Collaborating
- Complementing

Figure 6.1, the Coherence Model, summarises how these elements work together to develop a coherent version of PPI in research over time.

Fig. 6.1   Coherence Model

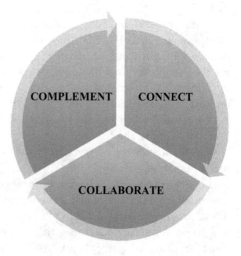

As this chapter progresses, we will show how the different elements of PPI involvement can be planned for and relate to each other to develop frameworks and pathways to decisions where PPI members of the research team can be involved and can co-produce research alongside other researchers. At the end of the chapter, we provide a checklist of the good practice points we have covered, that will help you plan and progress involvement in your future research.

6.1   CONNECTING

If we are to understand why and how people come together *to connect* in patient and public involvement, we need to understand the human motivations of both researchers and potential PPI members. As the German author Herman Hesse wrote in his poem 'Steps': 'A magic dwells in each beginning...' and as every relationship has a beginning, the magic of humanity plays an essential part in the way this may be achieved. It is important to clarify and confirm the researchers' motivations for wanting to involve lay members of the public (see also Chap. 1) which can vary from fulfilling funders' requirements, to recognising the value of expertise that comes from lived experience or from public views. They need to make this information readily available to members of the public who may want to become involved. However, equally, the researchers need to seek to understand what the motivations of members of the public may be. But lay members of the public themselves need to identify, understand and express their own motivations if they are to be able to negotiate their roles in research. Their motivations can be very different, ranging from altruism to acting through fellow feeling with others, to putting something back because of treatment or services they themselves or their families have received.

Making clear their own motivations will inform researchers' decisions as to who they may want to seek to involve, in what roles and at which stage of their research, whilst also shaping lay people's decisions on whether they wish to be involved with them. Doing this will help identify the most appropriate way for researchers to find lay people and for lay people to find them. For example, researchers may be better able to decide how and where to advertise, whether to organise introductory events inviting potential PPI members or whether to visit self-help groups. Understanding what the motivations of lay members of the public are may help researchers decide what they may need to offer to attract or support people to become involved. How will they meet and manage expectations and how will participants be selected?

Connecting requires resources and it is very important that they are realistically considered even before beginning to design a project. Resources refer not just to budget allocations but to practical resources such as time available to people, their health and skills as well as sense of efficacy and confidence that they can make a genuine contribution (see also Brodie et al. 2011).

In this section we will therefore consider:

- Finding each other: How can research and researchers engage lay members of the public? How can lay members of the public find research and researchers?
- Understanding each other: What do we expect and what can we expect?
- Agreeing the ground rules
- Allocating resources

6.1.1   Finding Each Other: How Can Research and Researchers Find Lay Members of the Public? How Can Lay Members of the Public Find Research and Researchers?

There are many ways for researchers to find people and for people to find researchers. The following section will describe four distinct ways of connecting with research from a general, open approach to a specific, personal one. We have called these: 'Prêt à PPI', 'generic', 'specific', 'outreach and inreach involvement'.

6.1.1.1   'Prêt à PPI': Starting with Ready-Made PPI Links

Some organisations and agencies have been set up, or have set themselves up, to recruit, prepare and help match people who have expressed an interest in being involved in research through PPI, with research teams and funders. This offers a ready-to-go, 'Prêt à PPI', way for researchers to access PPI groups and individuals quite quickly in terms of them being ready to recruit, and even more quickly if the organisations have provided some training about research to potential members of the public. This can also be a quicker way for people interested in becoming involved in research to make contact with researchers who want to recruit them.

Universities and funding bodies needing to get projects up and running within deadlines or to make contact with people from a wide range of areas or backgrounds often seek to work with individuals or agencies which they can employ to recruit people for them to take part in PPI. In England the Care Quality Commission, for example, issued a new procurement document in 2019 for a single contractor to deliver their 'expert by experience' services across England to enable them to involve 'experts by experience' in their inspection teams and co-production work. In their annual report for 2018/2019, they show that their expenditure with regard to experts by experience was just under £4 million, which was between 1% and 2% of their total expenditure. In some regions in England, clusters of local health service and research organisations have collaborated to pool resources and set up PPI member panels. In the county of Norfolk they have funded a Public and Patient Involvement in Research project (PPIRes) which started in 2003 and is still running more than twenty years later (Romero et al. 2016). This approach offers the benefits of potentially making quicker contact, although this may be at the expense of bypassing some aspects of relationship-building whereby people with different backgrounds and understandings of the research can get to know each other and identify what resources and skills they need to work well together in a research study or activity.

If PPI arrangements have to be set up very quickly to tight deadlines or if project partners' ambitions for involvement are modest, adopting a 'Prêt à PPI' approach may initially be effective. If an individual knows they want to become involved, but does not have much previous knowledge of the project they are engaging with, this 'Prêt à PPI' approach can also offer a good starting point by helping to get an initial PPI participant to help with finding others through their own contacts. However, there is a risk that this may lead to the recruitment of people with similar backgrounds and views. Short-circuiting important steps in connecting by starting in this way may merely defer issues that may then need to be identified and tackled further into the research.

6.1.1.2 *Generic: Starting with Non-specific Research Interests*
Another approach is for researchers to begin a *generic* search for PPI members without focusing too much on specific skills or knowledge such people should bring to the research in the first instance beyond the basics of the research topic. This approach would be useful if the research is interested in a community rather than a specific medical condition or

service, though even here the people would need to have experience of living in or working with the community concerned. We will now consider how to carry out such a search and what information researchers may need to provide for it to be productive both for recruiting potential PPI members and also to help to develop good relationships and involvement from the start.

Researchers or aspiring PPI members can search using websites and social media, local networks or local media, posters or leaflets in surgeries or hospitals, through voluntary sector and community groups, by organising events and of course by word of mouth. They may also speak to community leaders.

The information that researchers need to provide about their topic, project or programme should outline the subject of the research activity, what it seeks to achieve, why and how people might want to become involved and what difference their involvement would make. Even in such a generic search, it is important to show how the researchers' approach will be inclusive; for example, the promotional information should make it clear that the researchers are genuinely seeking everyone's views, including those who may openly challenge current thinking, and that those who may require extra resources to become involved are invited. It needs to state whether venues are wheelchair-accessible, whether sign language interpreters can be provided, whether reasonable adjustments can be made and support provided such as payments for childcare to enable people to participate. Involvement principles should apply in *generic* searching but are also essential in the *specific* searching we describe in the section that follows.

6.1.1.3 Specific
Some projects may need to involve PPI members who have specific skills or knowledge and this will require more *specific* ways of searching. Of course, this approach will depend heavily on the nature of the research and the skills that may therefore be appropriate. There are at least three avenues that can be explored for finding such people. The first is to look for people who have previously been involved in similar projects or for their family, carers or friends. The second is to identify organisations or professional bodies that work in that specific area, such as treating cancer or otherwise supporting people living with the condition, or caring for people living with dementia. They may include hospitals, community services and GPs; charities or voluntary organisations; but also self-help groups.

All of these may be able to help to identify service users and their carers. The third is to contact social and geographical groupings. If the research is about young people, researchers may consider approaching schools and colleges or youth groups that young people attend. If the project focuses on a geographical area such as a coastal community, researchers may want to contact the local authority to see if they do work in local communities and already have contacts, or, as these communities are often deprived, researchers could work with community development organisations. Alternatively, they could contact the local population directly through leafleting relevant neighbourhoods or organise local engagement events.

A striking example of a research programme arising from long-term collaboration between specifically interested lay and scientific groups is that of the US-based National Breast Cancer Coalition of breast cancer advocate, activist and support groups, which came to influence philanthropic funding decisions, breast cancer and environmental policymaking over many years. This brought together providers, scientists, consumers and policymakers to powerfully shape priorities for research funding, design and public reporting of findings (Osuch et al. 2012). A clear feature of the support to enable lay members to have an effective voice at the highest level to make changes was the intensive four-day training programme they provided and their use of participatory methods.

Unlike in a *generic* search where anybody interested and able will be invited to become involved, a specific approach often targets people who may not initially be interested or may not be able to take part without assistance. In such a search, the information provided needs to be even more specific, to explain more precisely what sorts of experience and skills people may need to bring to the research and why these are essential. It will be especially important to be clear about what adjustments will be made to enable people, perhaps with specific disabilities or medical conditions, to be involved. It is absolutely essential to acknowledge that people's time is an extremely valuable resource, especially if they are living with a medical condition or are caring for a relative or friend.

6.1.1.4 Outreach and Inreach Involvement

This section is about specific ways of involving lay members of the public who may be less likely to become involved through the other three approaches. It is important to start by considering why this may be the case. Of course, news of the opportunity may simply not have reached them, so it is important to advertise in a wide enough range of media and groups, targeting those that the people you need to reach are most likely to use. However, even if people are aware of an opportunity they may not take it up for reasons of resources, motivation or other difficulties such as lack of confidence, lack of physical access, negative previous experiences or fear of negative effects such as losing benefits or being rejected. They may, for example, be ex-offenders, or people stigmatised through medical conditions or something in their personal background. The people they are seeking may be socially or physically excluded from groups or places, or overlooked within them. This approach requires researchers to identify the barriers and analyse their nature and then plan deliberate, skilled and suitably resourced activities to overcome them.

An outreach approach would encourage more engagement through one or more members of a research organisation going out to places in the community and meeting people in order to build relationships. Outreach activities such as pop-up stalls or workshops in public spaces may be needed to contact and reassure people who have been physically or socially excluded.

Inreach, by comparison, is an approach in which a research organisation seeks to strengthen their engagement with communities by actively encouraging those communities to have closer relationships and contacts with its own activities and resources. Inreach working may be needed to contact and reassure people who may be physically or socially overlooked even though physically present in relevant groups or localities. It may mean providing individuals or teams with the right experience and interpersonal skills to spend time focusing on these groups or localities or to provide activities that are different from those normally available. Working in this way may bring rewards later in the research process as PPI members grow in confidence. Here is an example where a combination of inreach and outreach approaches might be helpful.

Case Example 7   Engaging Carers
Unpaid carers, people who stay at home to look after a member of their family, are difficult to involve because they often have little contact with the outside world, lack the time to be involved and may lack confidence if they have been caring for some time. Today the views of carers are considered increasingly important when services for people who are suffering from medical conditions or are old or frail are being redesigned. It may be possible to contact them through a specific search involving organisations that provide support for them or are treating a person for whom they are the named carer. However, this

(*continued*)

Case Example 7   (continued)
may have limited success as the carers often feel that they really do not have the time. Therefore a combination of inreach and outreach approaches may be more successful. There are many groups arranged by organisations or volunteers where carers can meet regularly to get advice and support, and, just as importantly, have a break from their responsibilities. Attending these groups would enable researchers to meet carers face to face and explain exactly what they want to do and how they intend to go about it. However, they need to be aware that they are infringing on precious time. An additional approach would be to have a stall in a specialist fair for carers or in a place that all carers will go eventually such as a market, supermarket, shopping mall or open public space where they can start to engage with the carers. The researchers need to be precise in the information they present. First of all they need to be very clear about the subject and scope of the research so that a carer can understand how the outcomes will affect them personally or the person they are caring for. Secondly they need to explain the process and the time commitment, so that the carers can consider whether what they are being invited to do is achievable. Based on these conversations, researchers may wish to consider alternative approaches. And finally, researchers need to talk openly about the adjustments that can be made, including funding alternative care arrangements while the carer is absent, covering other expenses and advice on the effect of any payments on benefits. This, together with some gentle encouragement, should help carers to make an informed decision.

6.1.2   Understanding Each Other: What Do We Expect and What Can We Expect?

The process of researchers and PPI members starting to understand each other should, with a few exceptions, have already begun when people started to find each other, for example, through information provided on posters or handouts, or conversations in meetings. However, further steps to gain and exchange information will be needed to achieve a proper understanding so that the working relationship can be planned and then managed. Time needs to be allowed to understand everyone's needs and expectations and build a working relationship that matches these. This can best be achieved by hosting at least one exploratory face-to-face meeting where people can express to each other what they as individuals are expecting and what they can expect from each other. If possible everyone involved should have their responsibilities and commitments confirmed in writing to help them decide if this is the kind of PPI involvement they can work with; this will be a document to which they can refer later. This should happen at some time before the induction meeting.

6.1.2.1 *Motivations*

We have raised the importance of people's motivation throughout this book. At the stage when plans for involvement are being put in place, people wanting to contribute as PPI members of the research team often state that they want to become involved in PPI to 'give something back'. Behind this simple statement lie complex personal stories and reasons for wishing to be involved ranging from simple altruism to acting through fellow feeling with others, reciprocating something they or a member of their family or a friend have received such as specialist care or support, or insights they have into how treatment or services work. Some may want to find ways to apply time, energy and skills they have; others may want to help others in a similar situation but who do not have the time, energy and skills to be involved themselves; and yet others may simply be seeking a purpose for themselves. All these reasons are absolutely valid but the better they can be spelled out and understood, the better they can be addressed when collaborating in involvement. Researchers will also need to have explained and if necessary clarified their rationale for seeking mutual involvement in PPI. Both PPI members' and researchers' motivations need to be explored in some detail to help them work together; in this way they can hopefully ensure that either the expectations arising from the motivations of both can be met or at least everyone knows which ones cannot be met so that people can decide whether or not to continue, or are prepared so that they will not be disappointed later. Making clear what motivations people may have and which ones may or cannot be addressed will help conversations about the expectations of PPI that may need to be carefully managed. We now go on to look at these.

6.1.2.2 Expectations

Researchers should be able to clearly explain what they expect a PPI member to be able to do within a particular research project, for example: how much time they may need to commit for reading; when and where meetings will be; and whether information exchanged may need to be treated in confidence and not shared outside meetings or team members. In the early stages of involvement, PPI participants can often state that they do not have particular expectations. However, research on volunteering in general has shown that there are some common, almost universal expectations which are highly significant for people giving their time. When asked what they got out of volunteering, volunteers in the public sector stated 'making a difference', 'enjoyment' and a 'sense of personal achievement' as the most important (McGarvey et al. 2020). While only about half of volunteers said that recognition was important, 90% felt that they had 'received enough recognition' suggesting recognition may also be a significant expectation (Low et al. 2007). Making such expectations clear from the outset gives a means for reviewing how these are or are not being met over time and at the end of any research project, and in turn how this may have contributed to PPI involvement being good quality.

6.1.2.3 Decisions

Having found each other, exchanged information about each other's aims, motivations, expectations, characteristics, needs and the resources available, the time comes to decide whether or not it is right for everyone to go ahead with being involved. Is the prospective PPI member confident that this team and area of research is right for them and do they have a mindset that will enable them to collaborate in this research? For example, are they open to learning about the pressures researchers need to manage, and are they themselves willing to be challenged? Are researchers clear about their responsibilities to support PPI members to express different views to each other and the research team? If both researchers and PPI members agree, it may be very helpful to set out motivations and expectations in a document which lists responsibilities and commitments. This should happen during the set-up phase. It is, however, important to recognise that trying to formalise this may be counterproductive if you want to involve types of group or individual that are difficult to involve as seen in Sect. 6.1.1.4. In this case, you would need to consider carefully what is suitable.

6.1.3   Agreeing the Ground Rules

We have so far seen many reasons why transparency is important for helping to build collaborations with a PPI contribution. Given the explicit aim of PPI partnerships to bring together people with differences in views, and potentially power, an agreed set of ground rules needs to underpin formal patient and public involvement. If this is not in place, someone needs to ask why not. The precise form and type of ground rules may differ according to the type of activity, such as workshops or management meetings, but they should all be chosen on the basis that they are relevant, appropriate and will progress the overarching principles of involvement. Thus, ground rules designed for a single deliberative workshop may be verbally agreed, but those that will apply throughout a project will probably need to be set out in writing, to refer to the policies of the organisation in which the project will be run and to be made available to lay members and researchers as they join the project. Three basic underlying principles for ground rules on which to base genuine PPI involvement are particularly helpful and can be summarised as mutual respect, accessibility and safe spaces, which we discuss here in turn.

The first principle, *mutual respect,* means that nobody should be treated simply as being there to serve the purposes of another person, to be used. This should be reflected in how tasks are allocated; in the general style and content of communications, including how meetings are chaired; and how people's contributions are received and recognised.

The second fundamental principle is about guaranteeing real *access,* whether physical or in terms of the language used. It cannot be acceptable to arrange meetings or to communicate in a way that makes people feel uncomfortable or excluded, especially if the needs were identified in the earlier stages we have already considered. This principle applies to roles at all levels within the research structure from lay members of the steering group to those attending deliberative workshops and PPI participants.

The third is about *creating safe spaces.* Everyone involved needs to be able to express themselves freely without fear of repercussions and with a safe means to address concerns. This requires, for example, strict confidentiality about what people discuss where necessary, and providing support for people so that they are open to accepting the different views of others, but also a process for dealing with complaints about what happens in the process of PPI involvement. We now look at applying these principles in more detail.

6.1.3.1 Access

A discussion of access requires recognition of at least three areas: physical, psychological and communication.

Physical access relates to all the usual facilities of a venue: for example, whether there are steps to negotiate, suitable disabled toilets or a hearing loop. It also refers to the location, for example how easy it is for everyone to get there and whether there is regular public transport at the times of meetings. It also refers to the timing of meetings, for example can people with children or caring responsibilities who want to attend make the times for which the meetings are arranged.

Psychological access is about having an environment that is enabling and welcoming for everyone. People should be routinely greeted and made welcome, instead of being left alone or in separate groups; not everybody is sufficiently confident to introduce themselves at first. The way in which the meeting is run should not be intimidating or patronising, as this could well make less experienced members fear that a contribution from them would not be taken seriously. It is good practice for the person chairing a meeting to be aware of who is or is not speaking and invite those individuals who are quieter if they would like to add anything.

> *Case Example 8   Being Overwhelmed by Experts*
> An academic colleague, Tony (not their real name), who has a particular health condition was invited onto a panel that makes funding decisions about research in the area of that health condition. The colleague did not know what to expect but on entering the room quickly realised that the panel members were mostly highly-qualified senior specialists in treating this condition, who knew each other well. Despite their having considerable academic experience themselves, Tony did not feel able to take part in the specialist-dominated discussion. The meeting was therefore not accessible to someone without specialist qualifications.

Communication is primarily about language in its widest sense. At its most basic, it is about whether people who do not have the majority language as their first language can take part. In this sense, it relates to national and regional languages or the use of sign language. It also relates to the technical language and terminology or jargon used in relation to various professional specialisms. However, language can also be used to remove or share power or social status in discussions and decisions. We will need to ensure that lay members' contributions are judged as valid or useful even if the way in which they express themselves is different from that of other project members, especially if they have disabilities related to communication. Communication can be organised to take account of and manage such differences positively and sensitively, providing interpreting or translations into different languages, using simpler language, speaking more slowly or clearly, or providing easy-read formats. Written documents need to be pitched at a level that is accessible to all those concerned in the research.

All of these access issues point towards means of redressing power imbalances between team members including PPI participants.

6.1.3.2 Power

Projects can never avoid power imbalances, and the balance of power may shift over the duration of a project as different people's skills and team positions are viewed as having particular value or where some responsibilities are given priority. Everyone in a project can take a view on whether to seek to review and rebalance the value attributed to relative contributions. It would be wrong to assume that only PPI members of the research team may feel disempowered and it is important to speak openly about how people are viewed and how they seem to view each other, perhaps reflecting unconscious biases within the project. Empowering members of the team is not just a question of adopting procedures and rules or giving voting rights. Empowering requires people to be able to reflect on their own experiences and have a chance to learn and to express what they need to participate, see Sect. 6.2.1.2.

For example, a regional research programme invited PPI members to join the board as lay representatives. The meetings were infrequent and a lot of work went on in between which was not presented in the meeting papers. At a briefing session for PPI members from across the programme to discuss their role, the lay board members reported that they found it difficult to contribute, not because of the seniority of the board members but because they did not have sufficient access to information on the topics under discussion.

Exercising power irresponsibly can lead to many types of harm and to reduced safety for people on the project team and those affected by the work of the project, so we now turn our attention to safety issues.

6.1.3.3 *Safety*

Attending to safety is about protecting PPI participants and researchers alike if things go wrong. While issues seen as calling for safeguarding measures and what safeguarding measures may be will vary between projects and organisations, the safeguarding policy already in place in the organisation where the project is based should be used as a first point of reference here. This should cover at a minimum issues such as confidentiality and compliance with data protection policies (such as the General Data Protection Regulations, GDPR), and having a whistle blower policy to allow anyone on the team to draw attention to anything they see which is dangerous or has already caused harm. However, as we saw in Chaps. 3 and 4, the specific topics and relationships covered by any given project may give rise to particular harms and therefore particular safety issues and risks to be managed both through and during PPI involvement.

6.1.4   *Allocating Resources*

As we have seen in previous chapters, different kinds of historical and political resources can enable or restrict PPI involvement. It would be a very big mistake to think that 'resources' applies only to planning the project budget for involvement. Of course, it is important to accurately estimate and to review the direct financial cost of involvement, whether through payments for involvement, travel costs or meeting costs, but the resources that will make a crucial difference between success and failure in involvement will be giving the right amounts of time for involvement and for building and sharing knowledge of and through involvement. However, we have to attend to managing relevant financial income and costs appropriately for each project to ensure that PPI finances are managed well. Project finances are usually managed by setting up a budget.

6.1.4.1 *Finance*

Any budget planned to cover PPI involvement costs will need to fit within the finance policies of whichever organisation is running a research project. Existing finance policies may restrict the way in which some funds can be spent on different types of costs. As PPI in research has become more usual, and indeed required, it has become possible to work out the direct costs of involvement within commonly used budget headings. In England, the NIHR INVOLVE organisation has developed an online calculator to help work out and present these direct costs. The calculator takes into account five categories: payment and rewards, expenses, involvement activities, involvement staffing and other costs. The first category of 'payment and rewards' covers involvement fees to individuals, vouchers or other incentives such as prize draws, donations to participating groups or networks, funding for additional training and for honorary appointments. The second category, 'expenses', lists travel, subsistence, childcare, carer costs, personal assistants, overnight accommodation and costs of any home office. Under the third category, 'involvement activities', it lists the cost of finding and training people, venues and catering, equipment and books as well as access to university and NHS facilities and conference fees. Under the fourth category, 'involvement staffing', the calculator recognises the cost of administrative support, involvement co-ordinators, independent facilitators and peer researchers. Finally under 'other costs', it looks at criminal record checks, translation and interpreting costs and support for people with physical or sensory disabilities. It also recognises that this list is not exhaustive.

However, as we recognised earlier, not all relevant resources relating to PPI involvement that call for planning will be financial. In the next three sub-sections, we look at time, skills and then health in terms of how PPI involvement plans for them.

6.1.4.2 Time

Any commitment to good PPI practice needs to recognise that a substantial amount of time will be required. Failure to build adequate time into the overall project plan is very likely to result in PPI adding to the workload pressure on researchers because it is neither preplanned nor systematic. This in turn will shape the way PPI activities can be delivered so that they are unlikely to achieve the best results. Allowing sufficient time for consultations to run or giving sufficient notice of meetings so that everyone needed can attend and arrive fully prepared can be seen to be fairer and to ensure fuller representation of views. This area of planning is often neglected and can mean that organisations will not meet their own policy guidelines on inclusive involvement. Planning how time is allocated will take account of the roles both researchers and PPI participants will need to fulfil if they are to collaborate and be fully and appropriately involved as set out early in the project. This will mean making explicit what activities need to be done and, importantly, drawing on the skills individuals are intended to contribute.

6.1.4.3 Skills

The ideals of PPI involvement in research aim to draw on and bring together the skills of both the researchers and the PPI members of the team, so as to build research that can be relevant and valid. However, training to deliver high-quality patient and public involvement is currently not part of the routine training for researchers or health and social care professionals. While an abundance of guidance is now available, this is not necessarily comprehensive or in many cases sufficiently specific to build useful skills. In the early stages of a project, training on the research process may be essential for PPI members working in a research environment, including the pressures that involvement places on academics who will need to manage it as part of the PPI collaboration. Training in all these areas can be seen as a direct benefit for both PPI members and researchers, and for the research project or programme. Over the period of a project, further training and skills development may be found to be appropriate and this too would need to be built into the project resources plan.

6.1.4.4 Health

It is a fundamental responsibility of the people leading a project to ensure that being involved does not put at risk or damage the health of either researchers or PPI members. For the researchers, who may already be protected by employment law and contracts, this may mean ensuring that workloads are achievable within the working hours allocated. However, everyone needs to ensure that the activities of PPI members of the research team, whose involvement is not covered in this way, are planned in such a way that it is clear what hours they, too, are being expected to contribute; what they are being expected to do can reasonably be fitted into that time; but also their contributions are matched to their health and energies; and the kinds of activities they are being involved in are not too exhausting or distressing. This may need particular care where PPI participants are being asked to be involved because they have experience of particular physical or mental health conditions, which can give rise to difficult memories or distressing insights into the kinds of challenges being faced by the subjects of the research study; and contribute their information as evidence. Where appropriate, this needs to be assessed in supervision, the regular review and information-sharing meetings between a PPI member and a named member of the research team who is responsible for them in their involvement activities, and adequate adjustments might need to be made.

Case Example 9   Effect of Meetings on Health

Jill has a health condition that means she gets easily exhausted and anxious but was repeatedly asked to attend two-hour meetings which also meant travelling to get to and to return from them. Jill says: "Go to meeting and be exhausted for the next week, or don't go". Attending those meetings affected her health severely but the research seemed unaware of this and the choice to attend was left to her. If Jill had been able to express her concern and if the team regularly checked with everyone involved for issues they might want to address, then the team could have come to discuss whether the meetings could be organized in a different way or explored with Jill some different options for accessing them which could be less tiring.

The UK's Social Research Association Ethical Guidelines (2003) explain that

The reputation of social research inevitably depends less on what professional bodies of social researchers assert about their ethical norms than on the actual conduct of individual researchers. In considering the methods, procedures, content and reporting of their enquiries, researchers should therefore try to ensure that they leave a research field in a state which permits further access by researchers in the future. (Page 23)

This applies equally and comprehensively to patient and public involvement; the underlying principle of involvement practice should be not only to protect participants from harm but also to ensure that they wish to continue to be involved in the current research and may join a new project in the future. In the next section, we consider the importance of these principles in helping everyone to collaborate.

6.2   COLLABORATING

Everyone involved is starting from the same standpoint, so collaborating does not happen as a matter of course. We need to understand that it is a process of relationship-building which enables people to co-operate to produce some outcomes on which they agree (Marinez-Moyano 2006). PPI involvement needs to be seen as this kind of active collaborative process. We have described earlier how and why a set-up phase is needed to confirm ground rules to manage expectations and agree to commitments. We have also seen how the key principle of medical research—'first do no harm' (*'primum nil nocere'*)—must also apply to patient and public involvement and be the most basic consideration throughout collaboration. Commitments need to clearly and explicitly extend to adopting practices that are not harmful, ensure that people are not excluded and are likely to continue to wish to collaborate.

Good collaborative practice demonstrates that people are valued. At an absolute minimum, researchers need to ensure that they are routinely respectful and polite, and mindful of others' needs for and while collaborating; a simple 'thank you' goes a long way. Such practices are not optional. Forgetting to behave in a way which is consistently collaborative may lead to willingness or enthusiasm for involvement on the part of PPI members going backwards. We do not see the greater involvement of PPI members as enabling researchers to avoid collaborative practices once the introductory phase is over, but rather as requiring continuing and active renewal and development of collaborative practices to meet any new and changing circumstances in which PPI members and researchers work together as the research develops.

In the next section, we will address a wide range of practical issues for building collaborative PPI which can be summarised as:

- Getting started: induction, training and payments associated with involvement
- Day to day: operational activities, valuing and dealing with problems
- Coming to the end: recognising, disseminating and continuing aspects of involvement

6.2.1   *Getting Started: Induction, Training and Payments Associated with Involvement*

Whenever people get to know each other, there is a starting point which can be crucial in determining whether what follows will go well or not, and the same applies to the process of getting involved in collaboration. Everyone who needs to be involved in collaborating will need to discuss and agree a range of issues which often cover some form of *induction, training* and *payments associated with involvement*. These could be aired and planned at an initial meeting limited to bringing PPI members of the research team together with the people who may have made initial contact with them to answer any queries they may have raised. It is absolutely essential to plan well for this meeting ensuring that people are not excluded from this decision-making process and checking to ensure the meeting is fully accessible, drawing on the knowledge gained in earlier contact conversations. This meeting will precede the induction process where everyone involved in the research will need to be included, and could include the discussion of perspectives and motivation.

6.2.1.1 Induction

The induction process requires the people leading the research to give all members of the team a comprehensive review of what they need to know about the project. This will follow the meeting at which expectations and motivations are clarified. It is likely to include information about the research organisation; the particular project and all the people involved in it; all relevant policies including health and safety and complaints; arrangements for supervision; and all relevant procedures such as claiming expenses. It should also include an introduction to evaluation. It will be helpful if members of the team collaborate to prepare a checklist of this information. Access should be made available to local and national guidance and handbooks. It will also be necessary to familiarise everybody with the wider environment in which the project will take place, such as relevant buildings or towns. Finally, it will be necessary to arrange identification including badges, if required, email access and shared online resources at this time. Helpful examples of shared online resources may be the English NHS Patient and Public Participation Policy (NHS England 2017a) and 'Working with our Patient and Public Voice (PPV) Partners – Reimbursing expenses and paying involvement payments (v2)' (NHS England 2017b).

In addition to providing information, this meeting will also provide an excellent opportunity to further build working relationships.

6.2.1.2 Training

The training needs of both researchers and the other people involved in PPI should be assessed at an early stage, soon after the induction meeting. In order to identify the training needs of individuals, it will be important to work out collaboratively what skills they may need to enable them to contribute meaningfully to the project based on the information they have been given at the induction meeting, what is unfamiliar and what gaps they have in their knowledge or skills. It is unlikely that everybody working in a given area will have the same skills set, so their training needs may vary. It is important to remember that there will be distinct roles within the project; this is not about turning PPI members into mini researchers but they do need to understand the basics of research. Everyone involved needs to understand and have appropriate access to the aims, activities and planned outcomes of the project. Helping people to gain confidence and skills is an essential contribution to empowering them to be actively involved, see Sect. 6.1.3.2.

6.2.1.3 Payments Associated with Involvement

Earlier we saw how to set the budget for involvement (Sect. 6.1.4.1). Once the project starts, systems for distributing the funds, for example to pay expenses, need to be put into place using the organisation's finance team. There are a range of potential pitfalls which must be taken very seriously and addressed. The one that probably raises most concerns is uncertainty about the effects of payments for involvement when people are receiving state benefits. In common with a number of countries, recent advice in England (NHS England 2017b) about involving people receiving state benefits, health insurance premiums or tax concessions, places the sole responsibility for any loss of benefits, exemptions or bonuses on the recipients:

> For the avoidance of doubt, it is the responsibility of the individual PPV Partner to comply with the conditions of their benefits, and not NHS England. (NHS England 2017b: 10)

However, we must remember that it is the responsibility of the researcher that no harm is done.

6.2.2   Day to Day: Operational Activities, Valuing and Dealing with Problems

In order to ensure that PPI participants can be appropriately involved as fully as possible in the work of the project, they need to understand properly what is required to enable the day-to-day activities in PPI to go forward. There are many lessons to be gained from established guidance for managing volunteers although the requirements for PPI participants may be somewhat different. Guidance provided within health services which involve volunteers, such as the NHS in the UK, commonly highlights that it is essential to enable volunteers to feel supported in *operational activities;* be recognised and therefore *valued;* have their needs met; and have issues and potential *problems* identified early (NHS England 2017c). In the UK, the

National Association of Voluntary Service Managers provides NHS employers with 'Guidelines for Volunteer Induction, Statutory and Mandatory Training' (Hall and Dring n.d.). The Directory of Social Change has published a very well-established and regarded 'The Complete Volunteer Management Handbook' (Jackson et al. 2019, now in its fourth edition). We now consider in more detail operational activities, valuing and dealing with problems in PPI.

6.2.2.1 Operational Activities

The basic requirement informing all operational activities should be that they reflect the principles and practice that have been agreed through working collaboratively as suggested in the first part of this chapter. PPI members should have a named contact who is regularly accessible. It will be helpful if the project organisation adopts a flexible approach towards PPI members that can adapt to everyone's changing needs, as well as processes for providing two-way feedback on work within the project, including supervision, and for raising and discussing issues of concern. If the project is large or takes place over a lengthy period, regular meetings to give updates and feedback may be useful.

If a collaborative approach is adopted to PPI action and interactions around PPI issues, it is likely to be unhelpful and counterproductive if team members try to hide behind set rules, regulations and processes which interrupt or block collaboration. We saw earlier in this chapter that when setting expectations people need to act in good faith and be willing to achieve the outcomes everybody is striving for. This does not mean wilfully breaking rules or abandoning research protocols, but it does mean being constantly aware of what is happening and changing and being prepared to openly adjust operational activities so that they meet everyone's purposes as opposed to trying to fit peoples' purposes to excessively rigid protocols.

6.2.2.2 Valuing

We can increase people's commitment to shared purposes and outcomes in a project if we ensure that everyone who contributes knows they are recognised and therefore *valued*. Throughout the operational life of a project, there should be times or processes designated for reflecting on the contribution that individuals make to the project. This includes not only PPI members and researchers but also administrative support or staff in other departments who are helping to implement good practice. *Valuing* can range from a simple 'Thank you' and recognising a task well performed, providing an example that people can follow elsewhere, to conferring engagement awards within the organisation.

6.2.2.3 Dealing with Problems

Dealing with problems is a critically important area which has in the past been insufficiently discussed. While it may feel difficult or disloyal to reveal problematic areas when working to achieve innovation in democratic inclusion, this cannot work well or be successful unless we understand what can go wrong; can identify and address such difficulties promptly; and permit anyone involved to raise concerns, not just those who belong to a particular group. This requires agreed policies and processes to be put in place for raising concerns, managing and resolving them, and working to achieve reconciliation, with responsibilities designated for each of these tasks.

While this empowers PPI members to raise concerns and have them listened to, the corollary is to deal sensitively with challenging or simply unacceptable behaviour on the part of PPI members; for example, someone might fail to respect confidentiality, or use inappropriate language, such as sexist or racist language. This also requires a process to be laid out in advance that may begin with a review discussion of the problem and giving support to the PPI member(s) involved, but may lead to a PPI member being asked to leave the project. As in all other activities, the principles of transparency and fairness must underpin whatever process is followed when discussing and responding to problems that may have been identified.

Case Example 10   Rights of Volunteers
The Volunteer Rights Enquiry undertaken by Volunteering England (2010, 2011) found that on occasions people felt mistreated or abused by the organisations they volunteered for but that they had no means to be heard. The committee members called on involving organisations to get it right from the beginning, for example by having policies and agreements in place, to have a clear process that allows for reconciliation, and for the involving organisation to take responsibility for putting this in place.

6.2.3   Coming to the End: Recognising, Disseminating and Continuing Aspects of Involvement

PPI involvement is not an abstract concept; it is about a group of people with different backgrounds and views collaborating to achieve particular outcomes for a project or programme with limits on its time or resources. At some point it will come to an end and this will need to be managed in such a way that those taking part can see how some of the experiences and outcomes they aimed for have been delivered. The approach can include *recognising* contributors and their contributions, *disseminating* findings and what has been learned, and then *continuing* aspects of the involvement if this is needed or valued.

Recognising the value of what they have done may be the minimum that some PPI members may have expected or wanted when they decided to be involved. Yet it is a sad truth that currently many researchers still need to be reminded that it is always good practice, and at the least common politeness, to let everybody who contributed their time and skills to a project know what the outcomes of their collaboration have been (Mathie et al. 2018). This is part of making involvement meaningful to everyone and will also demonstrate it is clearly recognised as having value. Good practice in research which is building knowledge for wider public use therefore also requires us to publicly *recognise* the contribution of those who have collaborated, including in any publications *disseminating* the experience and findings of the project.

6.2.3.1   Recognising

Earlier in this chapter, we described ways to *recognise* contributions of and to PPI while the project is under way, by showing appreciation and demonstrating that people are valued. In this section, we look at actions that recognise contributions when coming to the end of a project. Firstly, it is worth considering who the appropriate person or groups to express recognition will be: Should they come from the research project team itself, to confirm the value to the project; or should it be people outside the project team, such as the senior management of the organisation in which the project is based, perhaps confirming the value of such co-produced, impactful knowledge? Secondly, it is worth bearing in mind that as individuals are making PPI contributions based on their own personal experience, efforts and skills, it is important to name them and specify their contribution. Finally comes the issue of deciding how to provide such recognition. This can range from spoken tributes, personally or in a formal meeting, to certificates and awards to individuals, to written acknowledgements in academic or other publications, which we will now discuss in more detail.

6.2.3.2 Dissemination

The issue of disseminating findings at the end of a research project takes on particular prominence since published research findings are one of the main markers of successful research. This raises two issues for evaluating the contribution made by PPI. The first is to consider how PPI involvement can help give dissemination relevant reach and impact. The second is about acknowledging PPI in dissemination either in the 'Acknowledgements' section or as named co-authors if people have undertaken a role in the writing, both formally confirm PPI as central to producing a major research product. Furthermore, where findings from research influence services in ways which are meaningful for the networks of PPI members, they may be encouraged to be actively engaged in disseminating the findings. This is particularly the case where the research involves service improvements or the PPI members come from service user or community groups. These can be innovative. For example, a woman who took part in research on support for looked after children wrote a monologue about her experiences in adopting a difficult child. This was performed to a number of service providers.

PPI members may also be encouraged to engage in further PPI involvement because they realise that they can make substantial contributions to activities of real interest to them. This may include playing a leading role in drafting guidance for practitioners in applying and implementing research findings which have relevance for service user groups with which the PPI participants may have connections.

Good practice in academic publishing, from conference presentations to posters and peer-reviewed journal articles and monographs, makes it essential to be transparent about recognising contributions and co-authorship. The thesis resulting from PhD studies, in contrast, is a particular type of publication which cannot have co-authors as it is examined as the work of the individual student. However, if articles are published separately which cover specific areas of the PhD research study, partners can be credited if they are happy to state formally that the PhD student led and was clearly responsible for the work presented. Again, the division of responsibilities and how contributions can be acknowledged need to be clearly stated from the outset of people's involvement.

Disseminating academic findings may take years to complete as they are refined and peer-reviewed, but contributors should be regularly informed about any new instances of dissemination resulting from the project, and of course, their contributions should be acknowledged for any output where it was relevant.

We can find highly creative examples of lay groups shaping research dissemination as reported in the work of the Southern African Stroke Prevention Initiative (SASPI) in South Africa (Stuttaford et al. 2006). Here researchers, field workers and village communities came together to develop 'applied theatre' (*Xiseveseve*). This drew on African storytelling traditions which actively engage people in questioning and answering, to validate and disseminate stroke research findings in culturally meaningful ways and to co-develop further community interventions for stroke.

6.2.3.3 *Continuing Relationships*

The earlier section on finding PPI members and using UK Social Research Association guidance highlights how experienced PPI members may play increasingly significant roles in ongoing and future projects. As explained in the previous section, making sure that everybody knows about the outcomes of a project and who has contributed is an important step in enabling and helping PPI members to remain engaged in related projects. Other options for encouraging continued longer term involvement include inviting PPI partners to relevant meetings and events to disseminate findings, linking new projects to the original one, and developing research priorities.

6.3   COMPLEMENTING

The COHERENCE Model uses the term 'complementing' to describe activities that each contribute something additional and distinctive that fits in with and adds to the quality of the whole project or experience, and so complements it. In this section, we are focusing on how PPI involvement contributes to research and its outcomes.

However, even if every guideline in this book has been followed, simply including Patient and Public Involvement as part of research is no guarantee that the research output will be good, or achieve better outcomes for any change to current practice being tested. Even if the output is evaluated and is found to be effective or strongly challenges previous ideas, that does not mean that it will lead to changes in practice or attitudes. Even if implementing research leads to real change, this does not necessarily mean that the change will have the expected or predicted impact. And even if it leads to the expected or predicted impact, it may be impossible to compare the new practice with the one it has replaced through evaluation. These four premises need to be evaluated and acted upon to understand whether and how PPI makes any long-term difference to practice or research or whether it has a lasting impact, and to understand if findings about the topic or about the PPI contribution can be expressed in general terms.

Where, how and why each aspect of PPI may fit into involvement as a whole may be transparently summarised in a *logic model*; how this works in practice can then be *progressively evaluated* by reviewing the model; in this context it needs to be recognised that the formal end of a project is *not the end* of continuing contributions or the relevance of PPI.

One way to better understand PPI as an integral and complementary part of project planning and design requires an agreement between researchers and lay members which states clearly what they want to achieve with the project, why and how. One way to make what is being agreed and the reasons for this visible and checkable is to present it all in a *logic model*. Any such agreement should include any difference the involvement of lay members in the project is expected to make to the outcome.

In informing a *logic model*, such an agreement can guide how the research design can be matched with a suitable PPI design; all this will need to be reviewed at regular intervals. PPI members should, of course, be involved in the review.

Any agreement leading to a *logic model* will need to look beyond the completion of the project since, for example, it can take many years for some publications to be accepted or for the effects of changes in practice to be revealed. As we argued for dissemination, any plan must include means of keeping lay members informed and involved and crediting them suitably and respectfully, *progressively evaluating* their work, and engaging those who are experienced *beyond the end* of a given project.

This section will explore in more detail:

- Designing a pathway: building *a logic model*, outcomes and measures
- Following the pathway: regular reviews—*progressively evaluating*
- Beyond the end: deliberating, validation and continuation

6.3.1   *Designing a Pathway: Building a Logic Model Outcomes and Measures*

Designing a pathway for PPI is about setting out the key issues, putting them in context, understanding how they are related, agreeing the difference everyone wants to make and how this can be done with PPI involvement. These describe the basic requirements for a theory-led evaluation which goes beyond describing particular activities to evaluating their value or success. Such an evaluation is based on a theory which explains the purpose of the activities being evaluated, how they may be linked and reasons why they may lead to particular outcomes. Making all this clear to everyone involved in the evaluation means that they can better understand what is being evaluated and may be better able to check and reflect on progress and outcomes of projects and possible reasons why this has happened.

Theory-led evaluation can include evaluating PPI. Funders increasingly require a logic model to be included as part of any research application to clearly and logically describe to funders and researchers the difference the research project seeks to make and how it aims to achieve it. In the same way, good and transparent PPI practice will require a similar approach to understanding what everyone is contributing in order to make a difference and how their contributions can be enabled so that everyone involved can check on progress and outcomes. This means that a good *logic model* will require a means of describing the specific *outcomes* that are expected; how they will contribute to the bigger picture; how to evaluate whether or not those outcomes have been achieved; and often *how they will be measured*.

In practice, to plan for such an evaluation it will be necessary to put together a core group, which needs to include PPI members, to design it, carry it out and report back on progress and findings to the wider group.

6.3.1.1 Logic Models: Evaluating the Effects and Impact

A logic model is a means of setting out the steps required to test an idea (hypothesis) about a problem, and intended changes and effects in order to help to understand when testing the hypothesis whether the differences found are the ones expected or not.

Logic models were pioneered in the 1970s (for example by Carol Weiss 1972) and have since been applied in a wide range of approaches to studies to evaluate the impact of making changes using, for example, Theory of Change, Theory-Based Evaluation or Realist Evaluation, all of which are widely used in academic and community-based research. How to evaluate and the value of evaluation are still very much debated, but there is wide agreement that carefully applying an approach so as to understand what a project wants to achieve, why and how, will help reveal what difference it makes in the end. If those involved are found to be unfamiliar with the processes to be used, there will be a need for additional training, as described in the previous section.

Many practical guides to creating and applying logic models, in more or less detail and more or less mechanically or flexibly, are now available online, for example by NHS Health Scotland, NHS England Commissioning Support or NIHR RDS, and of course in print.

The model connects basic questions which look at how actions may be making changes to address problems as follows (see also Fig. 6.2):

- What is the problem?
- What difference(s) can be made to address the problem?
- What specific actions will help make that difference?
- How will we measure the effects (or outputs) of those specific actions?
- How can we assess what difference these effects have made (outcomes)?

There are many ways to record the connections between the answers to these questions, which are often seen as linear steps leading to *outcomes* and finally to *impact*. This approach can be used to improve understanding of PPI by connecting ideas and actions relating to PPI built into the design of a research project to the outcomes and impacts of PPI within the context of the evaluation of the research project itself. The following sections look further at evaluating outcomes and impact, particularly in relation to PPI. This is not often fully evaluated in any subject area, and where it is, it rarely involves PPI members. We aim, by this point in this book, to have provided information and approaches to support everyone involved in PPI to evaluate it. Figure 6.2 offers a graphic to describe a basic logic model.

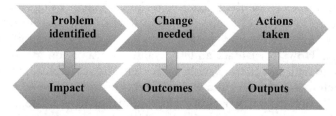

Fig. 6.2   Basic logic model

6.3.1.2   Outcome Framework

A logic model shows a set of detailed outcomes each linked to a set of specific steps each identifying what specific changes are needed to bring about the specific outcomes identified and located in the logic model; each of these sets of steps works like a mini-logic model, see Fig. 6.2. These are often recorded in tables for clarity. We have provided an example here showing steps linking general aims for PPI involvement to specific aims to outputs and through them to expected outcomes.

It is important to note that this template is not applicable to PPI in every project. Throughout this book, we have tried to provide ideas and information to help readers think about their own specific situation, aims, partners and projects and then work out for themselves what they need to set up and judge what PPI will be appropriate in their case. Table 6.1 illustrates how you might set up such a table after you have defined your aims and objectives collaboratively with all the partners involved. The following section looks more closely at ways of measuring *'outputs'* that reflect such outcomes.

Table 6.1 Example of objectives relating to an outcomes framework specific to the development of PPI in a research project

Aim	Specific aim for PPI members' involvement	Objectives to actively involve PPI members in roles
Meaningful involvement of patients and the public so as to improve knowledge	In setting research priorities	On funding panels
	In identifying research topics	In deliberative workshops
	In clarifying research question	On project steering group
	In research design	On project steering group
	In evaluation of the research process	On specialist advisory group
Meaningful involvement of patients and the public so as to improve methodology	In designing recruitment strategy	On project steering group
	In presenting proposal for ethical review	On specialist advisory group
	In designing patient- and public-facing materials	As consultants by honorary appointment
	In deliberating on themes emerging from data	On specialist advisory panel
	In determining findings	On project steering group
Meaningful involvement of patients and the public so as to improve democratic participation	Drawn from a range of backgrounds	Drawn from diverse backgrounds and actively involved
	Bringing specific experience	Bringing specific experience and actively involved
	Becoming committed collaborators	Continue in future projects and act as ambassadors for PPI activities

6.3.1.3 Outputs

The PPI outputs are the most visible because they are the most likely to be assessed using measurements of activities and how PPI participants' expectations have been matched; these can be agreed in advance, recorded and reviewed. They add to accountability within the project in general and in relation to how PPI has contributed in particular. In health and social care research, it is widely agreed that output measures must be collected consistently and transparently if they are to be seen to be accurate, relevant and worth monitoring and reviewing. As with outcomes, these are also often recorded and displayed in summary tables (see Table 6.2). They include measures such as: are invitations to meetings being sent in good time to support practical involvement; are requests for PPI comments being expressed in suitable language to engage PPI members; are PPI members given enough time to properly consider them; are PPI members being asked for their reflections on progress; and are PPI members being asked for their views and experience of involvement. As with

Table 6.2 Example of output measures relating to an outcomes framework

Aim	Specific aim	Objective	Output measure
Meaningful involvement of patients and the public in order to improve methodology	PPI members involved in designing recruitment strategy	Suitable PPI members are actively involved on project steering group.	PPI members receive documentation at agreed times Recruitment strategy is effective, achieves targets PPI members report satisfaction about process
	PPI members involved in presenting proposal for ethical review	Suitable PPI members are actively involved on specialist advisory panel	PPI members receive documentation at agreed times PPI members receive specialist training Project achieves ethics approval PPI members report satisfaction about process
	PPI members involved in design of patient- and public-facing materials	Suitable PPI members are actively involved as consultants by honorary appointment	PPI members receive documentation at agreed times Appropriate language services appointed, in time Community testing of materials completed and satisfactory PPI members report satisfaction about process

outcomes, we are not providing a standard template. We do, however, want to illustrate in Table 6.2 what kind of table you might want to agree to help you determine what you wish to measure and collect to reflect the aims and objectives of PPI in your project after collaboratively considering what is relevant for all your partners, that is, the people directly involved.

6.3.2   Following the Pathway: Regular Reviews—Progressively Evaluating

Rather than just addressing the question 'What makes a difference?' at the beginning and end of the project, one of the key elements of 'complementing' is regular review and learning along the way. The evaluation plan should include how often reviews will be undertaken, who will be involved and how, and what resources need to be allocated. It is important to remember that resources refer to time and skills as well as money. How this section is implemented will depend on how long the project is or, for example, whether it is part of a programme where the evaluation needs to run over several projects. The next steps are three core components of a progressive evaluation process. This is often illustrated as a cycle, but it can be helpful to see it as a linear process with a review at each key stage of a project.

6.3.2.1 Collaborating: Reviewing in a Team

As we noted earlier, a core group to carry out this part of the evaluation will need to have been confirmed at the outset, but we will still need to consider who else might need to be involved. Has the project reached new people who might also provide insights for understanding and acting on the findings? Are experts with particular knowledge, experiential or technical, required? The starting point for evaluation may be a written report, but rather than simply reviewing it, the team should have the chance to fully deliberate the interpretation and wider implications of the findings. Collaborating in PPI means working as a team at every stage, and not just commenting on something that has been written up, but again ensuring that everyone thoroughly deliberates on what is and should be included when reporting findings.

6.3.2.2 Communicate to Validate

Communicating evaluation findings is essential if we want PPI to add to their reliability and transparency, involving groups who have links to research participants for validation. The core group performing the evaluation therefore needs to ensure that results of their deliberations are fed back to all relevant people who have contributed to the evaluation both for comment and to validate them, in order to demonstrate that they have been thoroughly considered. This does not mean that everybody has to agree with the findings but that everyone involved can see that evidence has been clearly and transparently communicated so that it can be taken into consideration when deciding on the next steps in the evaluation.

6.3.2.3 Confirm and Begin Again

The final stage is for everyone involved in the project to review the effects of any proposed changes and/or any new learning. The project will therefore need to give enough time for deliberating to consider the next steps after which stage the evaluation process should begin again.

6.3.3   Beyond the End: Deliberating, Validating and Continuation

At the end of a project or evaluation process, it is essential to assess what the information collected means, and to formally review the logic model created at the beginning. We argue this needs to be done in evaluating the PPI experience and contribution as well as the research project as a whole. The section that follows divides this process into three: *deliberating, validating* and *continuation*.

6.3.3.1 Deliberating

When the project is well under way or comes to an end, the full logic model should be reviewed so as to understand what difference the project has made and may continue to make. This will involve transparently recording the evidence available from the measurements of the outputs, and considering them in order to judge how and to what extent the outputs have addressed the outcomes and what difference the outcomes have made. This will be carried out in the first instance by the core group so as to make initial sense of the findings and what they may mean.

6.3.3.2   Validating

In the previous section, we described how validation is achieved by feeding back to a particular group responsible for taking forward the ongoing progressive evaluation. At this final stage, a wide range of stakeholders needs to be included in validating the findings, ideally finding a way to cover everyone who has been involved in the work of the project. The focus here is on confirming that a wide range of people will share the project view on what the findings mean.

6.3.3.3   Continuing

'Continuing' at the end of the project in this instance means deciding on the appropriate next steps based on what the findings mean and disseminating this information so that they can be used. At a minimum, everyone involved in the project, of course including the PPI members, should be clearly informed about what the outcomes of the research and of the project activities have been, that the project has been completed and what the next steps will be.

PPI can bring additional and much-needed views and skills which *complement* those of others involved in the research process. This calls for the right *connections* to be made between the people involved, and between actions and ideas so that they can *collaborate* to change the thinking and actions during and following the research. We introduced the COHERENCE Model to show how we can all flexibly develop, use and respect our own and each other's skills to understand changes we may need to make in our own and others' working practices. The checklist we provide below offers a reminder of all the key areas that the COHERENCE Model helps us mobilise and reminds us where to find them in the chapter and also keywords linked to each area.

6.4   THE COHERENCE MODEL OF GOOD PRACTICE IN PPI INVOLVEMENT—AN INVOLVEMENT JOURNEY CHECKLIST

The journey we have travelled together in this book has been about equipping you to build skills, resources and means to critically evaluate PPI experiences and projects in health and social care research. Table 6.3 offers a checklist for the various stages of this journey.

Table 6.3 Involvement checklist

Section	Sub-section	Keywords to characterise activities
Connecting		
6.1.1 Finding each other	6.1.1.1 Prêt à PPI	Working with agencies
	6.1.1.2 In general	Promotion and information
	6.1.1.3 For specific skills	Promotion and information
	6.1.1.4 Outreach or inreach involvement	Outreach or inreach skilled activities
6.1.2 Understanding each other	6.1.2.1 Motivations	Deliberative workshops
	6.1.2.2 Expectations	Deliberative workshops
	6.1.2.3 Decisions	Formal agreements
6.1.3 Agreeing the ground rules	6.1.3.1 Access	Physical, psychological, communication
	6.1.3.2 Power	Biases, empowerment
	6.1.3.3 Safety	Safeguarding and whistleblowing
6.1.4 Allocating resources	6.1.4.1 Finance	Calculator, involvement payments
	6.1.4.2 Time	Planning
	6.1.4.3 Skills	Training
	6.1.4.4 Health	Safeguarding
Collaborating		
6.2.1 Getting started	6.2.1.1 Induction	Policies, health and safety
	6.2.1.2 Training	Empowerment
	6.2.1.3 Finance	Systems, negative effects
6.2.2 Day-to-day	6.2.2.1 Operational activities	Volunteer management
	6.2.1.2 Valuing	Collaborative practices, awards, involvement payments
	6.2.1.3 Dealing with problems	Complaints
6.2.3 Coming to the end	6.2.3.1 Recognition	Certificates
	6.2.3.2 Disseminating	Feedback
	6.2.3.3 Continuing	Personal data permissions
Complementing		
6.3.1 Designing a pathway	6.3.1.1 Logic model	Theory-based evaluation
	6.3.1.2 Outcomes	Outcomes framework

(continued)

Table 6.3 (continued)

Section	Sub-section	Keywords to characterise activities
	6.3.1.3 Outputs	Output measures
6.3.2 Following the pathway	6.3.2.1 Collaborate in a team	Progressively evaluating
	6.3.2.2 Communicate to validate	Participant validation
	6.3.2.3 Confirm and begin again	Learning
6.3.3 This is not the end	6.3.3.1 Wider deliberation	Deliberative workshops
	6.3.3.2 Wider validation	Validation of findings (community)
	6.3.3.3 Continue	Dissemination

REFERENCES

Brodie, E., Hughes, T., Jochum, V., Miller, S., Ockenden, N., & Warburton, D. (2011). *Pathways through participation: What creates and sustains active citizenship?* London: NCVO/IVR/involve.

Hall, J., & Dring, S. (n.d.). *Guidelines for volunteer induction, statutory and mandatory training.* The National Association of Voluntary Services Managers.

Jackson, R., Locke, M., Hogg, E., & Lynch, R. (2019). *The complete volunteer management handbook* (4th ed.). London: Directory of Social Change.

Low, N., Butt, S., Ellis Paine, A., & Smith, J. D. (2007). *Helping out: A national survey of volunteering and charitable giving.* London: Office of the Third Sector in the Cabinet Office.

Marinez-Moyano, I. J. (2006). Exploring the dynamics of collaboration in interorganizational settings. In S. Schuman (Ed.), *Creating a culture of collaboration* (p. 83). San Francisco: Jossey-Bass.

Mathie, E., Wythe, H., Munday, D., Millac, P., Rhodes, G., Roberts, N., et al. (2018). Reciprocal relationships and the importance of feedback in patient and public involvement: A mixed methods study. *Health Expectations, 21*(5), 899–908.

McGarvey, A., Jochum, V., Chan, O., Delaney, S., Young, R., & Gillies, C. (2020). *Time well spent: Volunteering in the public sector.* London: NCVO.

NHS England. (2017a). *Patient and public participation policy.* Redditch: NHS England.

NHS England. (2017b). *NHS patient and public participation policy, 'working with our patient and public voice (PPV) partners – Reimbursing expenses and paying involvement payments (v2)'.* Redditch: NHS England.

NHS England. (2017c). *Recruiting and managing volunteers in NHS providers, a practical guide.* Redditch: NHS England.

Osuch, J. R., Silk, K., Price, C., Barlow, J., Miller, K., Hernick, A., & Fonfa, A. (2012). A historical perspective on breast cancer activism in the United States: From education and support to partnership in scientific research. *Journal of Women's Health, 21*(3), 355–362.

Romero, J., Tracy Shalom, T., Kate Massey, K., Jeremy Dearling, J., Penny Vicary, P., & Abi Dennington-Price, A. (2016). *Public & patient involvement in research (PPIRes) a 12 year collaboration [Poster].* Norfolk and Suffolk Primary and Community Care Research Office.

Social Research Association. (2003). *Ethical guidelines.* London: Social Research Association.

Stuttaford, M., Bryanston, C., Hundt, G. L., Connor, M., Thorogood, M., & Tollman, S. (2006). Use of applied theatre in health research dissemination and data validation: A pilot study from South Africa. *Health (London), 10*(1), 31–45.

Volunteering England. (2010). *Volunteer rights inquiry: Interim report.* London: Volunteering England.

Volunteering England. (2011). *Volunteer rights inquiry: Recommendations and call to action.* London: Volunteering England.

Weiss, C. H. (1972). *Evaluation research: Methods for assessing program effectiveness.* Englewood Cliffs: Prentice Hall.

CHAPTER 7

Conclusion

The relationship between the public and providers of health services and research has been greatly transformed over two centuries by the efforts of many concerned groups to effect change. We can contrast earlier vigorous attempts by a growing medical profession to gain wider acknowledgement for their superiority, with more recent widespread social expectations of many groups to be included in health services and research decision-making. So, for instance, the Medical Journal boldly asserted in 1833 that 'the time is at hand when the respect due to our profession will be duly estimated and when interested tradesmen, clerks and shopkeepers—men of narrow ignorant minds—will, as governors, be divested of their insolence and impertinence to their superiors' (Brown 2009). This contrasts dramatically with findings of a recent study by Beighton, Victor and Carey et al. (2019) of the experiences of members of the public with learning disabilities involved in research, where a participant (P3) could confidently note:

> *"We, we are actually being listened to and taken note of. Our opinions counted taken seriously."* (P3)

P3 can be seen to be supported to make participation something to be experienced as of right. We hope this book has been right for you. We hope, also, that the exercise you completed at the very beginning, to help you decide whether to use this book, prepared you for what it is about: not just knowing the methods and practices of PPI but understanding your own motivation, perspective and commitment. We hope

© The Author(s) 2020

J. Grotz et al., *Patient and Public Involvement in Health and Social Care Research*, https://doi.org/10.1007/978-3-030-55289-3_7

you have engaged with our argument that there is no single right path to good PPI and that the path you take depends on you and how you choose to be involved.

In this chapter, we come to the end of our journey together, to explore patient and public involvement in health and social care research and to prepare you to plan your own PPI journeys. The book has aimed to offer something rather different from simply providing you with information about PPI, but instead to equip you to actively take it forward, by identifying ways for you to align your own ideas, practices, circumstances and research partnerships. Central to this approach is to move away from one person or group 'involving' another, towards everyone being 'involved with' everyone else in a way which recognizes comparable but different contributions, and in turn asks for everyone involved to find out how they can be personally committed to all of those they may be involved with through a research activity or project. This means promoting inclusion and working together in a coherent way to find supportive and enjoyable ways of being involved.

Health and social care research topics often concern difficult circumstances. So we have underlined that, to ensure people with experience of these can be involved to make research findings relevant to them, we need to take care to build both enjoyment and respect into our working relationships. We have also highlighted that developing respectful relationships, which encourage shared learning and research outcomes, require power to be shared between PPI volunteers and researchers. We have therefore tried to identify many ways of sharing and building power to advance these purposes.

This book, perhaps unexpectedly for some, does not skate over difficulties and tensions that can arise through involvement. Instead, we have explained how collaboration can be better when we recognize that making new partnerships can be disruptive, especially if existing practices exclude some people who may want to be included, and that changes may be resisted. We have therefore considered how, in building good PPI, we may need to make, hear and use criticism to good and constructive effect.

The preceding chapters have shown PPI in research as a process of involving people as a relationship, with constantly changing levels and types of involvement. Chapter 1 identified that for people to act differently in becoming involved, they need to take personal responsibility and build their own understanding about and comfort in their involvement role. Chapter 2 described a history of patient and public involvement relationships and policy which showed them as continually evolving, in the context of other social, economic and cultural changes. Chapter 3 explained why and how involvement relationships in research would need to take into account a context of diverse ideas, concerns and practicalities. Chapter 4 showed how the dynamics and actions of involvement relationships must centrally consider ethical obligations and the legal frameworks which govern them. Chapter 5 suggested how involvement is centrally concerned with breaking down 'us and them' dynamics, but that being able to listen to and express critical views must be part of this. Chapter 6 drew all of these elements together within the conceptual framework of the COHERENCE Model to equip us to flexibly develop and respect skills and to understand the changes that PPI requires in the organisation and outcomes of health and social care research.

One of the stereotypes of PPI practice we have therefore sought to question is the notion that involving people might simply mean bringing particular categories of people together in a place or meeting. We have shown how this aspect of involvement does not automatically ensure that viewpoints will be represented and articulated. Instead, we have seen that to meaningfully include diverse groups in research, so bringing distinctive experiences, may require us to learn to put in place unfamiliar processes of contact, discussion, negotiation and means of supporting active and equal contributions to research decision-making. We have looked at ways in which PPI can go beyond bringing 'us' to 'them' or indeed bringing 'them' to 'us', to taking working with 'all of us' as the reference point for developing topics and evidence. Taking this approach distributes responsibility for initiating PPI, for emergent research processes and for running research more inclusively, rather than leaving all of these to be led by an elite group.

We have also drawn attention and given value to the practicalities of research. 'Good ideas', wherever they have originated, will still demand practical work, which has to involve members of the wider community if we want to translate them into acceptable, safe and relevant research projects that are likely to be implemented in practice. We have highlighted that such collaborative development cannot be bland, but will involve people using power to exercise rights, in some countries supported by laws, to influence decisions on how to evidence findings on health and social care and to govern research to produce such evidence.

To show how PPI is not a static set of given statements, we explored, in Chap. 2, the history of people's involvement in health and social care, where we saw how securing such involvement entailed successive struggles over powers to gain or keep control as the opening quotations in this chapter suggest.

To make progress here has required public and patient groups to adapt to take advantage of continually changing opportunities for involvement. Such opportunities have related to corresponding changes in public expectations, health and social care institutions and knowledge. Taking advantage of these changes has given differing groups ways to access power to advance important value-based goals and shape value-based, equitable decision-making. Within health and social care, PPI arose from widespread critiques of and some resistance to both medical and administrative professionals gaining power in allocating resources to services and research, but giving fewer such powers to patients and the members of the public most likely to be affected by those decisions.

However, we saw how this changed dramatically and perhaps unexpectedly when post-war changes across many countries promoted wider access and rights to health and social care resources than in previous arrangements, which had excluded more socially and economically disadvantaged people. Yet, while welfare state developments such as the UK's NHS widened access to services they did not also widen control of the system beyond that exercised by medics and government. Widening access to services was accompanied by fewer openings for the expertise of the public and service users to shape either services or research. It then took several decades of effort by patient and public groups to secure more entry points for such groups to shape these processes. This has been complicated further in the UK as health services have been made separately responsible to devolved governments in Scotland, Wales and Northern Ireland. Many unpredicted economic and social events in the twenty-first century as well as dramatic health changes, such as those caused by the coronavirus pandemic, have made it even harder to anticipate what directions of involvement might be feasible or might prioritise citizen input. What we can learn from the many changes PPI has engaged with over time, is how PPI must always keep actively identifying potential opportunities to be involved and making the case for inclusively involving the wider community in health and social care decision-making.

Considering how to identify and manage the practicalities of being collaboratively involved in research was the concern of Chap. 3. Here we underlined that it is essential to understand what processes should and have been put in place to plan for involving patients and members of the public in research while also safeguarding them. To play their part as fully involved partners, having confidence in what kinds of involvement they are building, PPI participants and those supporting collaboration need such processes to be transparently and accountably communicated.

Our approach throughout has been designed to equip PPI participants to build their own independent contributions to involvement. The examples, exercises and checklists are brought in to prompt thinking, both to engage you as readers, but also to encourage you to engage others in involvement. Starting from clear principles has hopefully provided means to understand what these might mean in practice in differing research projects and partnerships, to anticipate when and where, and to decide who to involve as participants and how. To do this inclusively, we started by considering all people interested and with direct experience as possible participants from an early stage. This may raise challenges in terms of being aware of what may be needed to treat different groups with appropriate care and respect. We have also aimed to be open about the possibility that things can go wrong and either to anticipate these or to find ways to deal with things when they do go wrong and to safeguard everyone involved.

Appreciating the importance of keeping people safe and also understanding the ethical principles that are legally in force worldwide around research, we aimed in Chap. 4 to build awareness of the issues that relate to including and excluding people from research and from research processes. We argued these are closely related to good research design in more sharply recognising what is appropriate to particular groups and populations. This is further related to maintaining inclusive practices, because safeguards that are not appropriate cannot work and therefore cannot make people safe. We concluded that, in order to take every relevant lay or stakeholder group into account, it is necessary to map specific PPI roles in ethical designs and processes, to ensure diverse viewpoints are considered and managed appropriately in all ethics review processes. We explained the legal principles which might inform and support PPI contributions to such processes, but also identified social practices which can support their power to articulate their viewpoints and to better ensure we can recognise issues and practicalities that are relevant to the community in doing so.

PPI ideals aspire to more inclusivity. In Chap. 5 we identified that this also means not being too quick to exclude the many critical views surrounding PPI principles and practice. Instead, we can seek to understand the reasons for people holding such critical views. We argued that we need to do this if we want to go beyond the many discussions of PPI that are polarized, as Rose and Kalathil (2019) have argued. This is because otherwise we may have too readily excluded the viewpoints of some groups we need to include, whether service user groups, researchers or professionals. As discussions and activities concerning PPI practice have shown ways to persist with addressing differences, they have provided practical demonstrations for seriously thinking about this and acting differently within research partnerships. The advantages of disrupting the 'us and them' dynamic are now becoming more commonly recognised in a variety of political and conceptual discourses. We suggested ways to consider the criticisms of PPI and within PPI as helping us to appreciate them as part of the creative and dynamic context of diverse ideas and needs which shape PPI.

The interconnecting approach taken in this book was brought together in Chap. 6 which combined conceptual and practical insights and lessons within a COHERENCE model for PPI from which to decide appropriate next steps for generating and disseminating useful research project outcomes, keeping everyone involved informed about what the next steps may be. The road map for our PPI journey was illustrated in a conceptual framework to provide a reference resource for planning PPI involvement actions, presented transparently as a way of reviewing the lessons learned along the path traced by the earlier chapters of this book. We have argued throughout the book that PPI relies on valuing views and skills which complement those of others involved in the research process. This calls for the right connections to be made between the people involved, and between actions and ideas so that they can collaborate to change the thinking and actions during and following the research. We developed the conceptual framework of the COHERENCE model to show how we can all flexibly use and respect our own and each others' skills to understand changes we may need to make in our own and others' working practices. We suggested thinking about these in terms of a journey in stages that correspond to stages for developing research starting with early meetings bringing together, or seeking out, researchers and PPI participants; then coming to know about each other; then moving on to turning plans into research actions together, from start up to disseminating findings, which may call for more and other collaborations; and finally making sense of and aligning what we do in PPI within the overall context of research, its uses and its users.

We have described making connections not as something impersonal but as a whole-person, whole-system activity, relying on our taking care to recognise and draw on everyone's motivations and experience. While staying safe and keeping participants safe and free from harm must be attended to explicitly as the top priority, at every stage we need both to ensure and reassure people that we respect and review their wishes to become involved at each point. Motivations and experiences must be revisited and revised if necessary to check that people continue to wish to be involved in the current research. Doing this may help encourage experienced PPI members to be prepared to join a new project in the future, or to be clear when they do not, and to feel comfortable with this decision.

Collaboration cannot happen unless we understand that it requires a process of active relationship-building to enable people to produce some outcomes on which they have come to agree. Such relationship-building processes may include practices through which people can feel safe in acting and discussing, and which ensure that people are not excluded either deliberately or unintentionally.

Complementing, within the COHERENCE model, is a way of appreciating how difference, and diverse people and activities can bring additional and distinctive qualities which can fit within the whole project, or experience to bring higher quality, richer outcomes.

We have aimed throughout not to avoid but to recognize difficult topics and challenges in research projects and relationships, so as to find ways to actively address them. One such issue is the unavoidable existence of power imbalances. We have identified the skills and resources which can help shift balances of power or manage shifts that can happen during a project if some people's responsibilities or roles come to be valued differently relative to others. We have emphasized the usefulness of transparently reviewing and discussing political resources and how these may be managed in groups and settings which relate to research if we want to ensure equity of opportunities to contribute and to be listened to. Adopting procedures and rules or voting rights may be one way to do this formally, but we have also argued for applying principles of inclusion at every level for PPI contributions to be comprehensive and effective.

One underlying principle of good PPI, mutual respect, means never putting people in the situation of simply being there to be used by others but instead ensures tasks and responsibilities are allocated, communications designed, and people's contributions recognized equitably. A further principle of good PPI is to guarantee real 'access' to discussions, meetings, places so that arrangements support participation to be comfortable and inclusive of explicitly considered needs. The third principle of good PPI practice is related to access and is about creating safe spaces where participants are able to express themselves freely without fear of repercussions, and having processes to address concerns and complaints about the ways of being involved.

The emphasis we have placed on acknowledging and gaining means to deal with problems contrasts with the rather limited attention often paid to this in the PPI literature. We have not underlined criticism because of a wish to underplay the notable benefits or achievements of PPI in health and social care and research, but because we argue that being able to engage in criticism is essential to innovate and to demonstrate democratic inclusion. This approach supports anyone involved, not simply privileged groups, to raise concerns and questions and ultimately collaborate in shaping evidence-building policies and processes. Rochester (2013) has identified the importance of 'contentious action' in mobilizing voluntary groups and networks if they are to bring about changes for community benefit. We hope we have offered ways to encourage such action consistently throughout the book since learning about the PPI contribution must mean being prepared to disagree with accepted ideas and practices and being open to difference, while finding ways to manage them. This book has sought to encourage anyone interested in the role of patient and public involvement in improving health and social care and research, to take active steps to align PPI roles to their own circumstances and research projects, and to do so by deliberately building inclusive collaborations as safe and enjoyable.

The journey we have travelled together in this book has been about equipping you to build skills, resources and means to critically evaluate PPI experiences and projects in health and social care research. We hope what has been offered in this way will help you travel with more confidence on your own PPI journeys in the continuously changing circumstances and contexts for research and for involvement.

REFERENCES

Beighton, C., Victor, C., Carey, I. M., Hosking, F., DeWilde, S., Cook, D. G., Manners, P., & Harris, T. (2019). 'I'm sure we made it a better study…': Experiences of adults with intellectual disabilities and parent carers of patient and public involvement in a health research study. *Journal of Intellectual Disabilities, 23*(1), 78–96.

Brown, M. (2009). Medicine, reform and the 'end' of charity in early nineteenth-century England. *The English Historical Review, CXXIV*(511), 1353–1388.

Rochester, C. (2013). *Rediscovering voluntary action*. Basingstoke: Palgrave Macmillan.

Rose, D. S., & Kalathil, J. (2019). Power, privilege and knowledge: The untenable promise of co-production in mental 'health'. *Frontiers in Sociology, 4*(JUL), 1–11. [57].

GLOSSARY

Advisory panel is a group of people assembled to inform an organisation or project. Members of advisory panels have expert knowledge of the research topic and can offer an independent view. They are usually not directly involved in the part of the organisation covered by the research or the project itself and are not paid.

British Medical Journal (BMJ) is a respected and often-quoted medical academic journal published by the British Medical Association. According to its website it is *"one of the world's oldest general medical journals … published its first weekly edition on 3 October 1840"*.

Care Quality Commission is an independent regulator of health and adult social care in England registering, monitoring, inspecting and rating health and care providers in institutions and in the community.

Carer in this book is used to describe people who look after a family member or friend who is ill or disabled. They are often described as unpaid carers to distinguish them from paid staff, usually employed by care companies, who visit people in their own homes to provide care. Carer is carefully defined when applied to benefits such as the 'carer's allowance'. Organisations such as Carers UK provide information for unpaid carers on their website.

Carer support group(s) may be organised by voluntary organisations or the carers themselves. They are a form of mutual support where carers can have a break from their responsibilities, overcome isolation and often receive expert advice.

J. Grotz et al., *Patient and Public Involvement in Health and Social Care Research*, https://doi.org/10.1007/978-3-030-55289-3

Charitable organisation(s) are set up for public benefit with specific purposes which in the UK are defined by law and include 'relief of poverty', 'education' and 'the advancement of religion'. The Charity Commission for England and Wales has further information on their website.

Clinical commissioning group(s) were set up in law in England (see Health and Social Care Act 2012) to replace primary care trusts. They plan and commission health care services in their local area.

Community is a complex and debated term which generally requires context such as geography, ethnicity or shared experience, interest or work practice. It is debated because membership of specific communities is neither fixed nor automatically agreed. When we use the term in this book such as in 'community members', 'community services' or 'community organisations', we use it as shorthand for the many, various communities in the context of differing viewpoints about who can and should be seen as members.

Complementing is a term used in this book in a specific way as a part of the COHERENCE MODEL to describe activities that PPI and other project members bring, that each contribute something additional and distinctive that fits in with and adds to the overall quality of the whole project or experience, and so complements it (see Chap. 6).

Co-production (co-produced) refers to the inclusion of patients and service users on an equitable basis in designing or redesigning health and care services and research, to contribute their knowledge. It can be seen as contentious in that it represents only one development approach among several, because many patient and service user groups believe that this should be the accepted method of service and research development. We have provided some references in this book which relate to it (see Beresford 2019 in Chap. 5 and Rose 2019 in Chap. 6). For a short theory of knowledge, see also Beresford 2003 in Chap. 1.

Deliberative workshop(s) are a creative research method. They enable participants to have informed discussions about specific questions leading to the production of additional knowledge.

Dissemination captures a great variety of activities designed to transfer knowledge and information on the findings usually of a specific project or programme. In the context of this book, it ranges from publishing papers in peer-reviewed academic journals to policy briefings, conferences and plain English summaries and press releases.

Engagement is a complex and contentious term in the context of developing research (see Chap. 1). A broad definition is currently captured by the work of The National Co-ordination Centre for Public Engagement (NCCPE), an organisation which provides engagement information on its website and is funded by a range of key relevant bodies such as UK Research and Innovation (UKRI), Research England, the Wellcome Trust, and devolved Higher Education funding bodies.

Ethics are the philosophical ideas which we refer to, identifying the moral principles we need to follow in choosing and planning our actions and then deciding how we should act in practice. We deal with ethics comprehensively in Chap. 4 (see also Research Ethics and Research Ethics Committee).

Evaluation in this book describes the systematic assessment of the quality of outcomes of activities, projects or programmes, including for patient and public involvement (see Chap. 6).

Expert advisor is a term used, for example, by NHS England to describe PPI members with a high level of expertise relevant to a topic area in services or research who work alongside various other types of expert, often in advisory panels or steering groups. According to NHS England current guidance, they can receive involvement payments (see Chap. 3).

Expert by experience is a term used by a wide range of organisations from NHS England to the Care Quality Commission specifically to refer to people who have direct, first-hand experience of a service or research topic, thus distinguishing them from 'patients and the public' whose experience may be more general. Expert by experience can be a helpful descriptive term, but in the experience of the authors of this book, it has been rejected by some of the people involved in PPI in favour of other terms such as 'Patient and Service User Representatives'. It is best practice to check with people when we are discussing or working with them to find out how they want to be referred to.

Governance is a term for the defined system of how decisions are being made within an organisation or project, for example how their management groups are organised. (see, e.g. Research Ethics Committees which need lay members present to make decisions).

Health and Social Care Act (2012) is a law applicable in England which brought about a number of reforms to how the NHS in England is organised, for example through clinical commissioning groups and Health and Wellbeing Boards (see clinical commissioning groups and

Health and Wellbeing Boards). It also made PPI a legal requirement (see Patient and Public Involvement).

Health and Wellbeing Board(s) are hosted by local authorities in England bringing the NHS, public health, adult social care and children's services, elected representatives and Healthwatch together, to plan and co-ordinate services to meet the needs of their local population. They may, for example, challenge inequalities.

Health Research Authority (HRA) (The) reports directly to parliament under the Care Act 2014. According to its annual accounts 2018/2019, HRA works "with other organisations in the UK to regulate different aspects of health and social care research, ensuring research approvals and oversight are streamlined and proportionate... [HRA is] England-focussed but, through... joint working with the devolved administrations of Scotland, Wales and Northern Ireland, lead the oversight of health and social care research on behalf of the UK". It operates through jointly published key regulations such as the 'Governance arrangements for research ethics committees: 2018 edition'.

Healthwatch England reports directly to parliament under the Health and Social Care Act (2012) about the activities of the local Healthwatch organisations established in every area of England to "listen to and gather community views on services, and what to improve so as to share their views with those with the power to effects changes and help people find information on their local services, and to encourage services to involve people in decisions that affect them" (Healthwatch Annual Report 2017/18) (see also Health and Wellbeing Boards).

Impact is a term used in many policy and funding documents as part of a logic model (see logic model) to identify the overarching difference a programme or activity makes. It is distinct from outcomes (see outcomes) and outputs (see outputs) in referring to the wider effects of a programme or activity.

Inreach (involvement) is an approach in which a research organisation seeks to strengthen their engagement with communities by actively encouraging those communities to have closer relationships and contacts with its own activities and resources (see Chap. 6).

INVOLVE (NIHR INVOLVE) is an English national advisory group "established in 1996 and is part of, and funded by, the National Institute for Health Research, to support active public involvement in NHS, public health and social care research" (INVOLVE website).

Involvement in this book refers to a relationship when patients and the public move from being unquestioning recipients of services to being involved citizens, not just in decisions about their own care but in the planning and delivery of care for all and in the research to inform it. As there are many aspects and ways of involving, we need to carefully describe its context and purpose for each instance in which we use the term (see Chap. 1 for a comprehensive discussion).

King's Fund (The) is an independent charitable organisation working to improve health and care in England. They have published a range of research reports on health and care services which can be found on their website.

Lay representatives is a term often used interchangeably with other terms relating to patients and the public by a range of organisations when referring to people being involved. It connotes many other things in areas outside health and social care, for instance in a civil legal action, so it should be used wisely and the context in which it is being used should be explained.

Lay voices is a term used interchangeably with other descriptions of patients and the public by a range of organisations, when referring to people being involved (see, e.g. PPI members).

Logic model is a plan which shows a set of detailed outcomes together with a linked set of steps leading to delivering the associated specific changes needed to bring about each change. Each set of steps presents itself as a mini-logic model (see Chap. 6 for a fuller description).

National Health Service (NHS) Constitution for England was published in 2015. As the name suggests, it establishes key principles and values of NHS England.

National Institute for Health Research (NIHR) is a "virtual organization, mainly funded the Department of Health and Social Care whose work of supporting health and social care research spanning early translational research, clinical trials and applied research is hosted by NHS trusts, universities and life science organisations. Its programme is mainly focused on England but works closely with the devolved nations of Wales, Northern Ireland and Scotland. It also receives UK aid funding to support research for people in low- and middle-income countries" (NIHR website).

National Survivor User Network (NSUN) was set up early in the twenty-first century 'to build a more united and confident mental health service user movement' and was based on service user-led research, coordinated by Jan Wallcraft, which resulted in the report 'On Our Own Terms' in 2003. In 2013, they launched 4Pi national involvement standards.

Outcomes are the changes a research project is designed as intended to deliver.

Outcomes framework brings together the planned outcomes of a research project to provide the basis for a logic model (see above). Such frameworks are often recorded in tables to clearly present the steps and component parts as linked. We have provided an example specifically for PPI involvement in Chap. 6 which shows steps linking general aims for PPI involvement to specific aims to outputs and then to expected outcomes. Using an outcomes framework usually requires specialist training.

Output measure(s) help evaluate the products of activity of a project or organisation activities and may include simple accounts of numbers of participants and reporting of satisfaction but also the reach of services or research activities into previously excluded communities and the intended level and scope of dissemination.

Outreach involvement approaches encourage more engagement through one or more members of a research organisation going out to places in the community and meeting people in order to build relationships. Outreach activities such as pop-up stalls or workshops in public spaces may be needed to contact and reassure people who have been physically or socially excluded.

Participation is a term used sometimes interchangeably with 'involvement' or 'engagement' by various organisations, but the three terms may have opposing meanings. It is essential for us to establish how people who use it are defining it. In the context of research, it has at least two clearly opposing meanings which should not be confused. On the one hand, there is the context of 'participatory research' which encompasses a range of research methodologies in which power is deliberately shifted from the researchers to the people and communities affected by the research. On the other hand, a definition currently used by the NIHR refers to people's connection with a research project, having being recruited as research subjects to take part in clinical trials, or complete questionnaires, take part in focus groups or to provide their information in any other form of research data collection.

Patient and Public is the term used in this book to recognise that everyone will be a member of the public and a past or potential patient. This confirms that all those who we set out to involve have experience as patients and members of the public and so will have their own insights which draw on that perspective.

Patient and Public Involvement (PPI) is a term widely used but also continuously changing. It has no firmly agreed universal, fixed definition, and therefore on each occasion it is used, needs to be tailored to different contexts and its specific terms of use agreed. Involvement does not by itself guarantee a focus on inclusion. When we use the term in this book, we refer to the process of patients and the public moving from being unquestioning recipients of services to involved citizens not just in decisions about their own care or research but in the planning and delivery of care or research for all (see Chap. 1 for discussion and some common definitions).

Patient and Public Involvement in Research is very loosely described by the NIHR as "*research being carried out 'with' or 'by' members of the public rather than 'to', 'about' or 'for' them*". When we use it in this book, it follows from the way we use Patient and Public Involvement to contrast with passively accepting services as offered. Patient and public involvement in research, therefore, describes people moving from being unquestioning subjects of research to being involved members of a group undertaking research. In this case, patients and the public will be involved as volunteers, to improve the knowledge created and strengthen the design, having access to research meeting legal requirements and professional standards.

Patient and Public Voice (PPV) Partners is a term used, for example, by NHS England in specific guidance where it is defined as '*people who are willing to share their perspective and experience with NHS England to inform health services in a range of different ways*'. The term is used interchangeably with others. It is best practice to check with people how they want to be referred to and whether they see themselves as taking part in the organisation or project, so as to articulate their own or community members' viewpoints.

Patient participation group(s) are legally required in each GP practice in England to provide critical commentary on practice policies and issues relate to how services are delivered.

Power can be defined as the ability of individuals or groups to get others to do what they want them to do, even when those others do not want to do it. (see Chap. 4 Iphofen and Poland 1998: 19). In this book we provide many examples of how power is being used or might be shared in health and social care research.

PPI member is a term which implies that the individual is a member of a particular group in an organization or project where they have a designated PPI role comparable with other roles, perhaps professional or research-specific in the same body. The term is often used interchangeably with others. It is best practice to check with people how they want to be referred to and whether they see themselves as taking part in the organisation or project so as to fill a PPI-specific role.

PPI representative is a term which implies that the individual represents a particular group in a particular forum in the context of Patient and Public Involvement. The term is often used interchangeably with others. It is best practice to check with people how they want to be referred to and whether they see themselves as representing a group in the project where they have a PPI role.

Primary care is a service that provides a first point of contact in the healthcare system. They act as the 'front door' of the NHS and include general practice, community pharmacy, dental and optometry services, and other community-based services.

Public voice representatives is a term used, for example, by NHS England and is used interchangeably with other terms for Patient and Public Involvement. It is best practice to check with people how they want to be referred to.

Research Design Service, funded by NIHR, provides support to researchers in England, for example about writing grant applications and involving patients and the public.

Research Ethics were enshrined in law after abuses harmed research participants in the twentieth century. They require that all people taking part in research should only do so if they have given their fully informed consent. It also requires that all procedures planned and carried out in any research study have to be independently reviewed to ensure that they are ethical.

Research Ethics Committee(s) ensure that the ethics of a research project can be independently reviewed. They are responsible for protecting the rights to wellbeing of people involved in health research and of wider communities that may be affected by research outcomes. (See also Health Research Authority)

Service user(s) is a descriptive term for people who use support services including disabled people, people who use mental health services, people with learning disabilities, older people, and their families and carers and is used mainly in the context of social care. It is also a political term.

Some researchers suggest that a 'significant minority' would like to be referred to as service users. (See also Survivor)

Service user involvement means having people who use support services including disabled people, people who use mental health services, people with learning disabilities, older people, and their families and carers taking an active part in projects relating to them or in organisations that commission or provide them.

Stakeholder(s) is a generic term capturing anyone who may in any way be affected by or interested in the work of an organisation or project. The way in which the term is used varies with the organisation and the context and it is best practice to check who it includes. In addition, projects or organisations may need to regularly assess who their stakeholders are, what role they may play and how the project or organisation addresses their needs.

Statutory organisation(s) are established by Acts of Parliament in the UK, or other legislating bodies in other countries, often providing services paid for by the government such as the NHS and social care but also organisations which have duties to inspect or audit them, such as the Audit Commission or the Care Quality Commission.

Survivor is a term which can refer to surviving a medical condition. However, as with the term 'service user', it is not just a descriptive but also a political term to refer to a standpoint of surviving the system in which treatment is administered, against what some survivors see as their own best interest. See examples of information from the National Survivor User Network.

User-led is a term to describe organisations or projects mainly led by users of its service, or the service informed by a research topic. However, as with the terms 'service user' and 'survivor', it is not just a descriptive term but also a political term to support the idea of organisations controlled by people who use relevant support services. These may therefore include disabled people, people with mental health issues, people with learning disabilities, older people, and their families and carers. User-led services and projects may therefore campaign for more control of the support services they receive.

Voluntary sector is a generic term used to refer to a part of society that is different to the private and public sectors, and which can include charitable organisations, social enterprises and unregistered associations. The term is not sharply delineated and the sector is described by some as the 'large, loose and baggy monster'.

Volunteer, volunteering describes activities involving a commitment of time and energy which can take many forms. These activities are undertaken by choice and without concern for financial gain, conferring wider benefit, outside a volunteer's own family. Not everyone is likely to call such activities 'volunteering', therefore in the Community Life Survey amongst adults aged 16+ in England respondents are asked if they have provided unpaid help through groups, clubs and organisations. This is referred to as formal volunteering. The Community Life Survey identifies informal volunteering by asking about any unpaid help an individual may have given to other people, such as a neighbour, but not a relative, and not through a group, club or organisation. As the way people speak about volunteering varies greatly, it is very important to clarify what people mean when they use the term.

INDEX

A
Advisory panel, 51, 74

B
British Medical Journal (BMJ),
   17, 34, 98

C
Care Quality Commission, 107
Carer, 10–12, 36, 43, 47, 49, 54, 59,
   89, 108–111, 118
Carer support group(s), 6
Charitable organisation(s), 12, 21, 91
Clinical commissioning group(s), 7, 14
Community, 1–3, 7–9, 13, 14, 22,
   25–28, 30, 32, 33, 36–38, 43,
   44, 46, 47, 49, 55, 58, 59, 61,
   62, 67, 69–73, 76, 77, 79, 82,
   85, 91, 92, 95, 107–110, 127,
   128, 144, 145, 148
Complementing, 104, 128–137, 147
Co-production, 107

D
Deliberative workshop(s), 51,
   57, 62, 114
Dissemination, 8, 10, 50,
   56, 127–129

E
Engagement, 9, 10, 14, 41, 47, 85,
   96, 109, 110, 125
Ethics, 5, 7, 16, 42, 64, 65,
   67–82, 98, 145
Evaluation, viii, 35, 48,
   50–52, 57, 61, 62,
   99, 100, 122,
   129–132, 135–137
Expert advisor, 15, 51, 55, 56
Expert by experience, 107

G
Governance, 14, 28, 30, 43,
   50, 56, 57, 64,
   73–74, 92

© The Author(s) 2020
J. Grotz et al., *Patient and Public Involvement in Health and Social
Care Research*, https://doi.org/10.1007/978-3-030-55289-3

H
Health and Social Care Act (2012), 7
Health and Well-being Board(s), 8
Health Research Authority (HRA), 8,
    14, 68, 74, 75
Healthwatch, 8, 13–15, 32, 36

I
Impact, viii, 62, 80, 85, 88, 95–99,
    127, 129, 131–132
Inreach, 109–111
INVOLVE (NIHR INVOLVE), 10,
    13, 14, 48, 117
Involvement, vii–x, 1, 2, 4, 6, 7,
    9, 10, 12–18, 21–39, 41–44,
    47, 48, 50–66, 73–77, 82,
    85–101, 103, 105,
    107–114, 117–123,
    126–130, 132, 134,
    137–139, 142–146, 148

K
King's Fund (The), 18, 34, 101

L
Lay representatives, 11, 58, 90, 116
Lay voices, 11
Logic model, 129–132, 136

N
National Health Service (NHS)
    Constitution for England, 6
National Institute for Health Research
    (NIHR), 5, 8, 10, 13, 15–17, 42,
    43, 76, 77, 131
National Survivor User Network
    (NSUN), 33

O
Outcomes, vii, 5, 17, 71, 72, 79, 89,
    96–99, 111, 120, 123, 124, 126,
    128–132, 136, 137, 142, 143,
    146, 147
Outcomes framework, 133, 134
Output measure(s), 134
Outreach involvement, 109–111

P
Participation, 6, 9, 10, 32, 36, 41, 42,
    47, 61, 79, 141, 148
Patient and Public, 3, 11–12, 21,
    44, 95, 144
Patient and Public Involvement (PPI),
    vii–x, 1–19, 22, 24–26, 28–30,
    32, 35–38, 41–82, 85–101,
    103–108, 110–114,
    116–139, 141–148
Patient and Public Involvement in
    Research, viii, 2, 11, 13–18,
    41–82, 85–101, 103, 104,
    117, 142
Patient and Public Voice (PPV)
    Partners, 11, 38
Patient participation group(s), 36, 61
Power, viii, 3, 18, 22, 24,
    26–34, 37, 38, 68, 76,
    77, 79-81, 88, 90, 91, 93,
    94, 100, 114, 116,
    142–145, 147
PPI member, 7, 10, 44, 53,
    57, 60–63, 65, 69–71,
    77, 78, 80, 81, 87, 89,
    92, 96, 97, 105, 107,
    108, 110–113, 116, 119,
    121, 123–129, 131, 132,
    134, 137, 147
PPI representative, 1, 2, 5, 7, 11,
    12, 56, 57

Primary care, 6
Public voice representatives, 11

R
Research Design Service (RDS), 5
Research ethics, 5, 16, 67–82, 98
Research Ethics Committee(s) (REC),
    14, 73–75, 77, 78, 80

S
Service user involvement, 11
Service user(s), 4, 11, 15, 33, 38, 46,
    76, 77, 80, 86–88, 92–95, 97,
    101, 109, 127, 144, 146

Stakeholder(s), 8, 11, 29, 32, 47, 62,
    76, 78, 85, 86, 98, 99, 137, 145
Statutory organisation(s), 8,
    50, 53, 56

U
User-led, 12, 33, 94

V
Voluntary sector, 8, 108
Volunteer, 2, 12-18, 44, 47, 53, 64,
    65, 71, 73, 74, 76, 77, 85, 111,
    113, 123, 142
Volunteering, 3, 14–16, 113